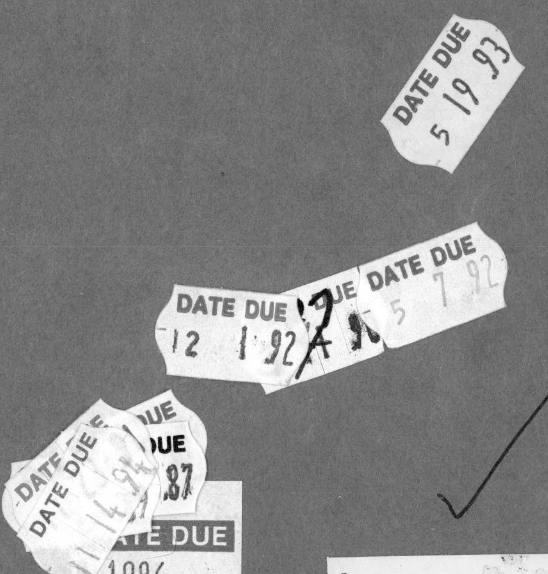
DATE DUE
5 19 93
DATE DUE
12 1 92
DATE DUE
5 7 92
DATE DUE
1986
DATE DUE
6 25 95

Stories for Free Children

Acknowledgments

Like It Is: Facts and Feelings about Handicaps from Kids Who Know, by Barbara Adams, photographs by James Stanfield. Copyright © 1979 by Barbara Adams and James Stanfield. Used with the permission of Walker and Company.

Is That Your Sister? by Sherry and Catherine Bunin. Copyright © 1976 by Sherry Bunin. Reprinted by permission of Pantheon Books, a Division of Random House, Inc.

X, by Lois Gould. Copyright © 1972 by Lois Gould. Reprinted by permission of Brandt & Brandt Literary Agents, Inc.

New Life, New Room, by June Jordan. Illustrated by Ray Cruz. Text copyright © 1975 by June Jordan. Illustrations © 1975 by Ray Cruz. Reprinted by permission of Thomas Y. Crowell Company.

A Few Cents More, by Sara D. Kash. Copyright © 1980 by Sara D. Kash. Reprinted with permission of the author.

What Is a Man? by Fernando Krahn. Copyright © 1972 by Fernando Krahn. Used by permission of Delacorte Press/Seymour Lawrence.

The Strange Voyage of Neptune's Car, by Joe Lasker. Copyright © 1977 by Joe Lasker. Reprinted by permission of Viking Penguin Inc.

Doctors for the People: Profiles of Six Who Serve, by Elizabeth Levy and Mara Miller. Copyright © 1977 by Elizabeth Levy and Mara Miller. Reprinted by permission of Alfred A. Knopf, Inc.

The Secret Soldier, by Ann McGovern. Copyright © 1975 by Ann McGovern. Reprinted by permission of Four Winds Press.

Peachy Pig, by Jane O'Reilly. Copyright © 1976 by Jane O'Reilly. Reprinted by permission of Wallace & Sheil Agency, Inc.

Beautiful My Mane in the Wind, by Catherine Petroski. Copyright © 1981 by Catherine Petroski. Originally published in *North American Review*.

The Princess and the Admiral, Copyright © 1974 by Charlotte Pomerantz. Originally published by Addison-Wesley Publishing Co.

My Day, Copyright © 1975 by Adele Aron Schwartz. Reprinted by permission of Harriet Wasserman Literary Agency, Inc.

My Brother Steven Is Retarded, by Harriet Langsom Sobol, photographed by Patricia Agre. Copyright © 1977 by Harriet Langsam Sobol. Photographs © 1977 by Patricia Agre. Reprinted with permission of Macmillan Publishing Co.

A Gun Is No Fun, by Shirley Camper Soman. Illustrations copyright © 1977 by Carlos Aguirre.

Three Strong Women: A Tall Tale from Japan, by Claus Stamm, illustrated by Kazue Mizumura. Copyright © 1962 by Claus Stamm and Kazue Mizumura. Reprinted by permission of Viking Penguin, Inc.

The Girl with the Incredible Feeling, by Elizabeth Swados. Copyright © 1976 by Elizabeth Swados. Originally published by Persea Books.

The Ten-Woman Bicycle, by Tricia Vita. Copyright © 1979, 1980 by Tricia Vita. Illustration © 1979, 1980 by Marion Crezee. Originally published by Sheba Feminist Publishers, 488 Kingsland Rd., London E84 AE, England.

Ira Sleeps Over, by Bernard Waber. Copyright © 1972 by Bernard Waber. Reprinted by permission of Houghton Mifflin Company.

The Story of Opal, by Opal Whiteley. Copyright © 1975 by Jane Boulton. Reprinted by permission of the editor.

STORIES FOR FREE CHILDREN

Edited and
with an Introduction by
LETTY COTTIN POGREBIN

A *Ms.* Book
McGraw-Hill Book Company
New York • St. Louis • San Francisco • Toronto

1 2 3 4 5 6 7 8 9 DOWDOW 8 7 6 5 4 3 2

ISBN 0-07-050389-3

LIBRARY OF CONGRESS CATALOGING IN PUBLICATION DATA

Main entry under title:

Stories for free children.
"A Ms. book."
Summary: A collection of short stories, fables, and fairy tales emphasizing non-sexist, multi-racial, multi-cultural themes.
1. Children's literature, American.
[1. Literature—Collections] I. Pogrebin, Letty Cottin.
PZ5.S8794 1982 [Fic] 82-9981
ISBN 0-07-050389-3 AACR2

Book design by Roberta Rezk

CONTENTS

This book is full of surprises: not only the surprising stories in it but some surprising stories *behind* it.

To many grown-ups, the biggest surprise may be that *Stories for Free Children* originated in *Ms. Magazine.* Of all the mass magazines and traditional women's magazines, only *Ms.*, regularly publishes a children's feature. A "Story for Free Children" has appeared nearly every month since our first issue came out in the spring of 1972. In fact, the collection you hold in your hands has been compiled in honor of the magazine's Tenth Anniversary.

For children, the biggest surprise about this book may be the discovery that *Stories for Free Children* was the inspiration for *Free to Be . . . You and Me.* Marlo Thomas, a *Ms.* charter subscriber, loved to read the magazine's children's stories to her niece, and went looking for similar fare in the bookstores. When she found that what she wanted didn't exist, she enlisted me and dozens of her friends who are writers, artists, composers and comedians to help her produce the book she had been searching for. In a wonderfully organic sense then, *Stories for Free Children* is both the parent and child of *Free to Be . . . You and Me,* having inspired it long ago and then following in its footsteps.

For me, the editor of *Stories for Free Children* from the start, the biggest surprise about this book has been the long demand for it. For ten years I have been receiving letters from readers who are fed up with conventional children's literature and thrilled to discover "the SFFC alternative."

Kids who tear out the stories and keep them in a looseleaf binder write that they want to replace their tear-sheet library with "a real book."

Each week's mail brings such letters as this, from a father in Seattle:

"As I read these stories to my children, I keep wishing I had heard them when I was growing up. They would have helped me feel a lot better about myself."

If we miss a month because of an occasional editorial space squeeze in the magazine, parents send us panicky letters like this one from a New Orleans mother:

"Whatever you do, don't omit the Story for Free Children! It's my daughter's only relief from passive princesses and ugly stepmothers."

Teachers tell us how they integrate the stories into the curriculum: they read them aloud to very young children; use them to initiate class discussion of difficult subjects such as divorce or gun control; add them to the reading lists for language arts, history, family living, social studies—and to college courses in psychology, sociology and Women's Studies.

Whether the letters come from teachers, parents or children themselves, so many of them end with the same request: "*Please make Stories for Free Children into a book.*"

And so we have.

But why all the fuss? What is so special about *Stories for Free Children*? What, for that matter, is a "free child?"

Very simply, you're a free child if you are allowed *to be yourself and be true to yourself.* That means being free to express the way you really feel, and to develop your talents and follow your own honest interests without having to measure up to other people's ideas of what a girl or boy is "supposed" to be.

It also means some *not*-to-be's: not feeling peculiar just because you might be different, not being afraid to say you're afraid, and not feeling ashamed if your life or your family seems less than perfect.

Free children grow up understanding that you can be many kinds of people in the same person. They like to like themselves *and* be just as positive about other people. They're happy playing with friends, but also when they're alone in a silence big enough to hide their secrets in. Sometimes they want to learn about the bad, sad things in life and sometimes they just want to be silly and have fun.

Stories for Free Children speak to all those many parts of a child. Furthermore, the same story sometimes says different things to different children: a story about an unemployed parent, for instance, may validate the reality of one child's life while to another child it introduces a new and enlarging fact about the adult world.

Young readers can open this book at random and be entertained, informed or challenged. For parents and teachers there is another option: you can pay attention to the way the stories are grouped—and why. Then you can choose the story you need when you need it: to affirm, to teach or to comfort.

In the section called Fables and Fairy Tales for Everyday Life, you'll find stories that both escape the bounds of the here and now and help children cope with their own here and now with fresh insight.

"The Princess Who Stood on Her Own Two Feet" shows how a tall princess learns that conformity can be crippling while the reward for authentic behavior is authentic love.

"Sun Stones" proves with mythic power that despair or boredom can be the mother of invention.

"Peachy Pig" and "A Magic Place" suggest that faraway adventure is as close as the nearest farmyard or city park.

Children who get energy and nourishment from having an imaginary identity will find themselves in the pages of "Beautiful My Mane in the Wind."

Besides funny rhymes and quirky images, "The Big Box" and "One Full Moon in June" offer two enlightening perspectives on freedom.

"The Princess and the Admiral," "Three Strong Women," and "The Ten-Woman Bicycle" reach back to a thirteenth-century kingdom, an ancient Japanese village and a nineteenth-century bicycle factory to reveal that there have always been women who are clever, mighty and brave. By introducing female counterparts to the awesome likes of Paul Bunyan, Kubla Khan and Thomas Edison, these new legends bring sex-equity to our dreams of greatness.

"X" exposes the foolish business of dividing humanity into pinks and blues, and does it in a form that combines parody, parable, mystery, fantasy, documentary, and science fiction into a genre all its own.

"What Is a Man?" and "The Girl with the Incredible Feeling" each seem to embody a prescription for the survival of the *self* among others. And their authors—Fernando Krahn and Elizabeth Swados—are people whose prescriptions for almost anything promise more interest than most.

Obviously, section two, Famous Women, Found Women, is not an equal opportunity collection. Its bias is frankly female because the rest of children's literature is so overwhelmingly, disproportionately male. A glance through any library's card catalogue will tell you that biography and autobiography has been largely a man's preserve, probably because until recently, interesting and exciting lives were available only to boys and men.

In traditional life stories, even the word used to identify the principle character is "genderized." *Hero* and *heroine* evoke different images: the hero fights the elements, solves the problem, leads the armies; the heroine is tied to the railroad tracks or locked in a tower awaiting the hero's rescue. But boldness, prowess, courage and valor are ultimately human virtures, so we do not need a female diminutive word to define a woman who has them. "Hero" will do.

Today, legions of female heroes are breaking barriers and breaking records in sports, science, politics, medicine and virtually every occupation. But there also have been exceptions in the past.

The stories in this section introduce a few such girls and women, some well known, others almost anonymous, but each audacious and admirable in her fashion. Just as both sexes are expected to draw inspiration from Abraham Lincoln's intrepid honesty and Martin Luther King's resolute visions, these female heroes are intended as models for both boys and girls.

From the "olden days," we meet *Deborah Sampson*, the secret soldier of the Revolutionary War; *Sybil Ludington*, the female Paul Revere; *Lucretia Mott* and *Amelia Bloomer*, who defied society and won new freedoms for women; *Mary Patten*, the young woman who commanded a clipper ship, navigating it through fifty-four days of stormy sea; *Opal Whitely* and *Edna Castle Little*, two "found women" whose ordinary lives give emotional texture to our sense of the past.

From our own generation there is *Dorothy Brown*, a doctor who is black, dedicated and outspoken; and ten tenacious girls who fought for the right to play in the Little League. Thus, this section—which began with an eighteenth-century woman who had to pretend to be a man in order to follow her talents—ends with our active, forthright twentieth-century daughters whose daily lives proclaim the uplifting declaration "*I can do it!*"

The last group of stories, Fun, Facts and Feelings, deals with everyday reality: the people children know, the circumstances of their lives, the problems they face and what they think and feel about it all.

Each subject is treated in a thoughtful and caring way, whether the theme is

violence ("A Gun Is No Fun"), a subtle treatment of child molestation ("I Like You to Make Jokes with Me, but . . ."), unemployment ("No Job for Mom"), sex discrimination ("A Few Cents More"), divorce and stepfamilies ("One Father, Two Fathers"), how to have fun though poor ("This Is a Picnic"), adoption ("Is That Your Sister?"), disability ("My Brother Steven Is Retarded" and "Like It Is"), the death of a child ("When Judy Died"), or the arrival of a new sibling ("New Life, New Room").

In this section too, there are stories that push against the boundaries of convention by revealing tacitly concealed truths about both sexes.

Instead of boys who have to be daredevils and act "cool" and tough to prove their manhood, here are stories about boys who take responsibility around the house ("Charlie Helps") and who discover that the need for security is universal ("Ira Sleeps Over").

Instead of girls who are doll-obsessed or boy-crazy, here are girls who are intelligent and sensitive in a strange culture ("This Is What I Know"), protective of their privacy ("Inside Out"), and stoic in the face of frustration ("My Day").

Stories for Free Children are multi-cultural, multi-racial and have a nonsexist point or purpose. But every story must also meet high literary standards. Among these is E. B. White's measure of good writing, a measure that counts most for authors whose audience is children:

"No one can write decently who is distrustful of the reader's intelligence, or whose attitude is patronizing."

And now, intelligent reader, let us turn the page and lose ourselves in a world that was or might have been—or find ourselves in a world that is just beginning.

Fables and Fairy Tales for Everyday Life

Part 1

X

By Lois Gould

Illustrated by Jacqueline Chwast

Once upon a time, a Baby named X was born. It was named X so that nobody could tell whether it was a boy or a girl.

Its parents could tell, of course, but they couldn't tell anybody else. They couldn't even tell Baby X—at least not until much, much later.

You see, it was all part of a very important Secret Scientific Xperiment, known officially as Project Baby X.

This Xperiment was going to cost Xactly 23 billion dollars and 72 cents. Which might seem like a lot for one Baby, even if it was an important Secret Scientific Xperimental Baby.

But when you remember the cost of strained carrots, stuffed bunnies, booster shots, 28 shiny quarters from the tooth fairy . . . you begin to see how it adds up.

Long before Baby X was born, the smartest scientists had to work out the secret details of the Xperiment, and to write the *Official Instruction Manual,* in secret code, for Baby X's parents, whoever they were.

These parents had to be selected very carefully. Thousands of people volunteered to take thousands of tests, with thousands of tricky questions.

Almost everybody failed because, it turned out, almost everybody wanted a boy or a girl, and not a Baby X at all.

Also, almost everybody thought a

Baby X would be more trouble than a boy or a girl. (They were right, too.)

There were families with grandparents named Milton and Agatha, who wanted the baby named Milton or Agatha instead of X, even if it *was* an X.

There were aunts who wanted to knit tiny dresses and uncles who wanted to send tiny baseball mitts.

Worst of all, there were families with other children who couldn't be trusted to keep a Secret. Not if they knew the Secret was worth 23 billion dollars and 72 cents—and all you had to do was take one little peek at Baby X in the bathtub to know what it was.

Finally, the scientists found the Joneses, who really wanted to raise an X more than any other kind of baby—no matter how much trouble it was.

The Joneses promised to take turns holding X, feeding X, and singing X to sleep.

And they promised never to hire any baby-sitters. The scientists knew that a baby-sitter would probably peek at X in the bathtub, too.

The day the Joneses brought their baby home, lots of friends and relatives came to see it. And the first thing they asked was what kind of a baby X was.

When the Joneses said, "It's an X!" nobody knew what to say.

They couldn't say, "Look at her cute little dimples!"

On the other hand, they couldn't say, "Look at his husky little biceps!"

And they didn't feel right about saying just plain "kitchy-coo."

The relatives all felt embarrassed about having an X in the family.

"People will think there's something wrong with it!" they whispered.

"Nonsense!" the Joneses said cheerfully. "What could possibly be wrong with this perfectly adorable X?"

Clearly, nothing at all was wrong.

Nevertheless, the cousins who had sent a tiny football helmet would not come and visit any more. And the neighbors who sent a pink-flowered romper suit pulled their shades down when the Joneses passed their house.

The *Official Instruction Manual* had warned the new parents that this would happen, so they didn't fret about it. Besides, they were too busy learning how to bring up Baby X.

Ms. and Mr. Jones had to be Xtra careful. If they kept bouncing it up in the air and saying how *strong* and *active* it was, they'd be treating it more like a boy than an X. But if all they did was cuddle it and kiss it and tell it how *sweet* and *dainty* it was, they'd be treating it more like a girl than an X.

On page 1654 of the *Official Instruction Manual,* the scientists prescribed: "plenty of bouncing and plenty of cuddling, *both.* X ought to be strong and sweet and active. Forget about *dainty* altogether."

There were other problems, too. Toys, for instance. And clothes. On his first shopping trip, Mr. Jones told the store clerk, "I need some things for a new baby." The clerk smiled and said, "Well, now, is it a boy or a girl?" "It's an X," Mr. Jones said, smiling back. But the clerk got all red in the face and said huffily, "In *that* case, I'm afraid I can't help you, sir."

Mr. Jones wandered the aisles trying to find what X needed. But everything was in sections marked BOYS or GIRLS: "Boys' Pajamas" and "Girls' Underwear" and "Boys' Fire Engines" and "Girls' Housekeeping Sets." Mr. Jones went home without buying anything for X.

That night he and Ms. Jones consulted page 2326 of the *Official Instruction Manual.* It said firmly: "Buy plenty of everything!"

So they bought all kinds of toys. A boy doll that made pee-pee and cried "Pa-Pa." And a girl doll that talked in three languages and said, "I am the Pres-i-dent of Gen-er-al Mo-tors."

They bought a storybook about a brave princess who rescued a handsome prince from his tower, and another one about a sister and brother who grew up to be a baseball star and a ballet star, and you had to guess which.

The head scientists of Project Baby X checked all their purchases and told them to keep up the good work. They also reminded the Joneses to see page 4629 of the *Manual,* where it said, "Never make Baby X feel *embarrassed* or *ashamed* about what it wants to play with. And if X gets dirty climbing rocks, never say, 'Nice little Xes don't get dirty climbing rocks.' "

Likewise, it said, "If X falls down and cries, never say, 'Brave little Xes don't cry.' Because, of course, nice little Xes *do* get dirty, and brave little Xes *do* cry. No matter how dirty X gets, or how hard it cries, don't worry. It's all part of the Xperiment."

Whenever the Joneses pushed Baby X's stroller in the park, smiling strangers would come over and coo: "Is that a boy or a girl?" The Joneses would smile back and say, "It's an X." The strangers would stop smiling then and often snarl something nasty—as if the Joneses had said something nasty to *them.*

Once a little girl grabbed X's shovel in the sandbox, and zonked X on the head with it. "Now, now, Tracy," the mother began to scold, "little girls mustn't hit little—" and she turned to ask X, "Are you a little boy or a little girl, dear?"

Mr. Jones, who was sitting near the sandbox, held his breath and crossed his fingers.

X smiled politely, even though X's head had never been zonked so hard in its life. "I'm a little X," said X.

"You're a *what?*" the lady exclaimed angrily. "You're a little b-r-a-t, you mean!"

"But little girls mustn't hit little Xes, either!" said X, retrieving the shovel with another polite smile. "What good's hitting, anyway?"

X's father finally X-haled, uncrossed his fingers, and grinned.

And at their next secret Project Baby X meeting, the scientists grinned, too. Baby X was doing fine.

But then it was time for X to start school. The Joneses were really worried about this, because school was even more full of rules for boys and girls, and there were no rules for Xes.

Teachers would tell boys to form a line, and girls to form another line.

There would be boys' games and girls' games, and boys' secrets and girls' secrets.

The school library would have a list of recommended books for girls, and a different list for boys.

There would even be a bathroom marked BOYS and another one marked GIRLS.

Pretty soon boys and girls would hardly talk to each other. What would happen to poor little X?

The Joneses spent weeks consulting their *Instruction Manual.*

There were 249 and one-half pages of advice under "First Day of School." Then they were all summoned to an Urgent Xtra Special Conference with the smart scientists of Project Baby X.

The scientists had to make sure that X's mother had taught X how to throw and catch a ball properly, and that X's father had been sure to teach X what to serve at a doll's tea party.

X had to know how to shoot marbles and jump rope and, most of all, what to say when the Other Children asked whether X was a Boy or a Girl.

Finally, X was ready.

X's teacher had promised that the class could line up alphabetically, instead of forming separate lines for boys and girls. And X had permission to use the principal's bathroom, because it wasn't marked anything except BATHROOM. But nobody could help X with the biggest problem of all—Other Children.

Nobody in X's class had ever known an X. Nobody had even heard grown-ups say, "Some of my best friends are Xes."

What would other children think? Would they make Xist jokes? Or would they make friends?

You couldn't tell what X was by its clothes. Overalls don't even button right to left, like girls' clothes, or left to right, like boys' clothes.

And did X have a girl's short haircut or a boy's long haircut?

As for the games X liked, either X played ball very well for a girl, or else played house very well for a boy.

The children tried to find out by asking X tricky questions, like, "Who's your favorite sports star?" X had two favorite sports stars: a girl jockey named Robyn Smith and a boy archery champion named Robin Hood.

Then they asked, "What's your favorite TV show?" And X said: "Lassie," which stars a girl dog played by a boy dog.

When X said its favorite toy was a doll, everyone decided that X must be a girl. But then X said the doll was really a robot, and that X had computerized it, and that it was programmed to bake fudge and then clean up the kitchen.

After X told them that, they gave up guessing what X was. All they knew was they'd sure like to see X's doll.

After school, X wanted to play with the other children. "How about shooting baskets in the gym?" X asked the girls. But all they did was make faces and giggle behind X's back.

"Boy, is *he* weird," whispered Jim to Joe.

"How about weaving some baskets in the arts and crafts room?" X asked the boys. But they all made faces and giggled behind X's back, too.

"Boy, is *she* weird," whispered Susie to Peggy.

That night, Ms. and Mr. Jones asked X how things had gone at school. X tried to smile, but there were two big tears in its eyes. "The lessons are okay," X began, "but . . ."

"But?" said Ms. Jones.

"The Other Children hate me," X whispered.

"Hate you?" said Mr. Jones.

X nodded, which made the two big tears roll down and splash on its overalls.

Once more, the Joneses reached for their *Instruction Manual.* Under "Other Children," it said:

"What did you Xpect? Other Children have to obey silly boy-girl rules, because their parents taught them to. Lucky X—you don't have rules at all! All you have to do is be yourself.

"P.S. We're not saying it'll be easy."

X liked being itself. But X cried a lot that night. So X's father held X tight, and cried a little, too. X's mother cheered them up with an Xciting story about an enchanted prince called Sleeping Handsome, who woke up when Princess Charming kissed him.

The next morning, they all felt much better, and little X went back to school with a brave smile and a clean pair of red and white checked overalls.

There was a seven-letter-word spelling bee in class that day. And a seven-lap boys' relay race in the gym. And a seven-layer-cake baking contest in the girls' kitchen corner.

X won the spelling bee. X also won the relay race.

And X almost won the baking contest, Xcept it forgot to light the oven. (Remember, nobody's perfect.)

One of the Other Children noticed something else, too. He said: "X doesn't care about winning. X just thinks it's fun playing boys' stuff *and* girls' stuff."

"Come to think of it," said another one of the Other Children, "X is having twice as much fun as we are!"

After school that day, the girl who beat X in the baking contest gave X a big slice of her winning cake.

And the boy X beat in the relay race asked X to race him home.

From then on, some really funny things began to happen.

Susie, who sat next to X, refused to wear pink dresses to school any more. She wanted red and white checked overalls—just like X's.

Overalls, she told her parents, were better for climbing monkey bars.

Then Jim, the class football nut, started wheeling his little sister's doll carriage around the football field.

He'd put on his entire football uniform, except for the helmet.

Then he'd put the helmet *in* the carriage, lovingly tucked under an old set of shoulder pads.

Then he'd jog around the field, pushing the carriage and singing "Rockabye Baby" to his helmet.

He said X did the same thing, so it must be okay. After all, X was now the team's star quarterback.

Susie's parents were horrified by her behavior, and Jim's parents were worried sick about his.

But the worst came when the twins, Joe and Peggy, decided to share everything with each other.

Peggy used Joe's hockey skates, and his microscope, and took half his newspaper route.

Joe used Peggy's needlepoint kit, and her cookbooks, and took two of her three baby-sitting jobs.

Peggy ran the lawn mower, and Joe ran the vacuum cleaner.

Their parents weren't one bit pleased with Peggy's science experiments, or with Joe's terrific needlepoint pillows.

They didn't care that Peggy mowed the lawn better, and that Joe vacuumed the carpet better.

In fact, they were furious. It's all

that little X's fault, they agreed. X doesn't know what it is, or what it's supposed to be! So X wants to mix everybody *else* up, too!

Peggy and Joe were forbidden to play with X any more. So was Susie, and then Jim, and then *all* the Other Children.

But it was too late: the Other Children stayed mixed-up and happy and free, and refused to go back to the way they'd been before X.

Finally, the parents held an emergency meeting to discuss "The X Problem."

They sent a report to the principal stating that X was a "bad influence," and demanding immediate action.

The Joneses, they said, should be *forced* to tell whether X was a boy or a girl. And X should be *forced* to behave like whichever it was.

If the Joneses refused to tell, the parents said, then X must take an Xamination. An Impartial Team of Xperts would Xtract the secret. Then X would start obeying all the old rules. Or else.

And if X turned out to be some kind of mixed-up misfit, then X must be Xpelled from school. Immediately! So that no little Xes would ever come to school again.

The principal was very upset. X, a bad influence? A mixed-up misfit? But X was a Xcellent student! X set a fine Xample! X was Xtraordinary!

X was president of the student council. X had won first prize in the art show, honorable mention in the science fair, and six events on field day, including the potato race.

Nevertheless, insisted the parents, X is a Problem Child. X is the Biggest Problem Child we have ever seen!

So the principal reluctantly notified X's parents and the Joneses reported this to the Project X scientists, who referred them to page 85769 of the *Instruction Manual.* "Sooner or later," it said, "X will have to be Xamined by an Impartial Team of Xperts.

"This may be the only way any of us will know for sure whether X is mixed up—or everyone else is."

At Xactly 9 o'clock the next day, X reported to the school health office. The principal, along with a committee from the Parents' Association, X's teacher, X's classmates, and Ms. and Mr. Jones, waited in the hall outside.

Inside, the Xperts had set up their famous testing machine: the Superpsychiamedicosocioculturometer. X

Nobody knew Xactly how the machine worked, but everybody knew that this examination would reveal Xactly what everyone wanted to know about X, but were afraid to ask.

It was terribly quiet in the hall. Almost spooky. They could hear very strange noises from the room.

There were buzzes.

And a beep or two.

And several bells.

An occasional light flashed under the door. Was it an X ray?

Through it all, you could hear the Xperts' voices, asking questions, and X's voice, answering answers.

I wouldn't like to be in X's overalls right now, the children thought.

At last, the door opened. Everyone crowded around to hear the results. X didn't look any different; in fact, X was smiling. But the Impartial Team of Xperts looked terrible. They looked as if they were crying!

"What happened?" everyone began shouting.

"Sssh," ssshed the principal. "The Xperts are trying to speak."

Wiping his eyes and clearing his throat, one Xpert began: "In our opinion," he whispered—you could tell he must be very upset—"in our opinion, young X here—"

"Yes? Yes?" shouted a parent.

"Young X," said the other Xpert, frowning, "is just about the *least* mixed-up child we've ever Xamined!" Xclaimed the two Xperts, together. Behind the closed door, the Superpsychiamedicosocioculturometer made a noise like a contented hum.

"Yay for X!" yelled one of the children. And then the others began yelling, too. Clapping and cheering and jumping up and down.

"SSSH!" SSShed the principal, but nobody did.

The Parents' Committee was angry and bewildered. How *could* X have passed the whole Xamination?

Didn't X have an *identity* problem? Wasn't X mixed up at *all?* Wasn't X *any* kind of a misfit?

How could it *not* be, when it didn't even *know* what it was?

"Don't you see?" asked the Xperts. "X isn't one bit mixed up! As for being a misfit—ridiculous! X knows perfectly well what it is! Don't you, X?" The Xperts winked. X winked back.

"But what *is* X?" shrieked Peggy and Joe's parents. "*We* still want to know what it is!"

"Ah, yes," said the Xperts, winking again. "Well, don't worry. You'll all know one of these days. And you won't need us to tell you."

"What? What do they mean?" Jim's parents grumbled suspiciously.

Susie and Peggy and Joe all answered at once. "They mean that by the time it matters which sex X is, it won't be a secret any more!"

With that, the Xperts reached out to hug Ms. and Mr. Jones. "If we ever have an X of our own," they whispered, "we sure hope you'll lend us your instruction manual."

Needless to say, the Joneses were very happy. The Project Baby X scientists were rather pleased, too. So were Susie, Jim, Peggy, Joe, and all the Other Children. Even the parents promised not to make any trouble.

Later that day, all X's friends put on their red and white checked overalls and went over to see X.

They found X in the backyard, playing with a very tiny baby that none of them had ever seen before.

The baby was wearing very tiny red and white checked overalls.

"How do you like our new baby?" X asked the Other Children proudly.

"It's got cute dimples," said Jim.

"It's got husky biceps, too," said Susie.

"What kind of baby is it?" asked Joe and Peggy.

X frowned at them. "Can't you tell?" Then X broke into a big, mischievous grin. *"It's a Y!"*

Lois Gould's most recent novels are La Presidenta *and* A Sea Change. *She is also the author of the collected essays* Not Responsible for Personal Articles.

the Princess and the Admiral

By Charlotte Pomerantz / Drawings by Tony Chen

This fable was suggested by an incident in the 13th century, involving Vietnam and the Imperial Navy of Kublai Khan.

A very long time ago, there was a small patch of dry land called the Tiny Kingdom. Most of its people were poor farmers or fisherfolk. Their bodies were lean and brown and strong from working long hours in the sun. They built the thatched mud huts in which they lived. They wove the simple earth-colored clothing they wore. And everyone, even the children, helped to plow the fields, harvest the rice, and catch the fish that they ate.

The land of the Tiny Kingdom was as poor as its people. The soil had neither gold nor silver, which was why no country, in the memory of the oldest man or woman, had ever made war against them. The people were good-humored about the poverty of the land. It had given them a hundred years of peace.

The ruler of the Tiny Kingdom was Mat Mat, a dark-eyed young princess, as lean and brown as her people. One night, almost a thousand years ago, the Princess looked out the window of her royal bedchamber at the fishing boats in the harbor below, then up at the pale sliver of a moon.

Tonight the young Princess was too excited to sleep. For this month marked the anniversary of One Hundred Years of Peace in the Tiny Kingdom. It would be celebrated, as were all great events, with a Carnival and Fireworks Display. Tomorrow morning, at the Council of Three Advisers, the Princess would choose the date.

There would be all kinds of firecrackers—flares, petards, and pinwheels that burst into flowers and waterfalls and fishes. Birds and butterflies would flit among trees of green fire. Then, at midnight, one—no, three—fantastic red dragons would slither and writhe across the night sky.

The next morning, the Princess was the first to arrive at the Council Chamber. The three advisers followed. First, the Elder, a man of ninety years. Then, the Younger, a man of eighty years. And finally, In-Between, who was exactly eighty-five.

The advisers were strangely silent and stonefaced.

The Elder broke the silence. "Excuse me, Your Highness, but there can be no peace celebration."

"Why not?" demanded the Princess.

"There are rumors of invasion," said the Younger.

"It looks like war," said In-Between.

The Princess stared at them, unbelieving. "But we have no enemies."

"I fear we do," said the Elder. "We have just had a report from our fishing boats that a large fleet of warships is at this very moment sailing toward our kingdom."

"How terrible!" said the Princess. "How many ships are coming?"

"Our fishing boats report twenty ships of war," said In-Between, "including the flagship of the Admiral."

"How large are the ships?"

"I would judge each to be about five times the size of the Royal Swan Boat," said the Elder.

"More like four times the size of the largest fishing boat," said the Younger.

"Mmm," said In-Between. "I'd say the truth lies somewhere in the middle."

"Never mind," said the Princess impatiently. "How long will it be before the enemy fleet reaches the harbor of the Tiny Kingdom?"

"Two days, more or less," the advisers replied.

The Princess settled herself on her throne. "Let us review our capabilities," she said, "and make some contingency plans."

The Elder spoke first. "We have no ships of war."

"We have no men or women under arms," said the Younger.

"We do have an inexhaustible supply of firecrackers," said In-Between. "Totally useless in the present emergency."

The Princess stepped down from her throne, walked to the window, and looked at the harbor below. "No forts, no soldiers, no weapons, no sinews of war," she mused. "Clearly, we shall have to rely on . . . other things." She walked briskly back to the throne. "Call in the Court Astrologer," she said.

The advisers shrugged. "With all due respect," said the Younger, "astrology is no substitute for weapons."

"We shall see," said the Princess.

An ancient and withered old woman tottered into the Council Chamber.

"Your Highness wants me?" she asked. "I haven't been consulted since your great-grandmother swallowed a chicken neck."

"I seek information about the position of the sun and the moon," said the Princess.

"With pleasure," said the old woman. "When the moon is in her first or third quarter, it's as if she were a stranger to the sun. But when she is a new moon or a full moon, there is a special, rather remarkable, attraction. We feel it on earth, in plants and oceans. I often feel it in my bones."

"And what of the moon tonight?"

"Tonight it is a new moon that hangs her fragile lantern over your Tiny Kingdom."

"Interesting," said the Princess.

She beckoned her three advisers to come close. "Our course is clear," she said. "As clear as the lantern moon." The four of them huddled together while the Princess whispered her plan.

"And so," she concluded, "the first order of business is to send out a dozen of our fishing boats to tease the enemy. Their ships will chase ours, and if all goes well, the enemy ships should get here at the right time."

The next day, upon orders of Princess Mat Mat, hundreds of farmers, fisherfolk, and children gathered in a nearby forest to cut down the tallest trees. The strongest men and women sawed through the trunks. The less strong sharpened both ends of the fallen trees, and the children stripped off the branches.

Then everyone helped to haul the tree poles to the riverbed. When the tide had gone down enough for them to drag the poles into the water, they hammered them—dozens and dozens of them—into the muddy bottom of the riverbed.

The Princess watched from the window of her royal bedchamber. When she had counted 253 poles jutting out of the water like a crazy, staggered picket fence, she gave orders for the people to return to their huts.

The next morning, when the Princess and her advisers stood on the Royal Balcony, not a single pole was visible.

"I thought the tide would be higher," said the Elder.

"I thought it would be lower," said the Younger.

"Your Highness," said In-Between, "I think you guessed just right."

"It was no guess," said the Princess. "Not after I talked to the Court Astrologer. We know the tides are caused by the attraction of the sun and the moon.

Therefore, when I learned that these two celestial bodies are especially close at this time, I knew that the tides would be exceptionally high. High enough to cover the tree poles." She smiled. "The moon is a faithful ally."

Just then, the first ships of the enemy fleet were sighted approaching the mouth of the riverbed. They were in full chase of the twelve fishing boats that had been sent out to tease them.

The enemy fleet sailed up the middle of the river. As they faced the village, fifty more fishing boats appeared from all directions and surrounded them.

Aboard the enemy flagship, the Admiral gave the command: *"Furl sails and drop anchor! Get ready to fight!"*

From the Royal Balcony the Princess looked down at the enemy ships and clapped her hands. "He did it! The Admiral did just what I hoped he would do!" she exclaimed, trying hard not to jump up and down.

On the river, the Admiral peered uneasily at all the fishing boats. "It looks as if they are going to climb aboard."

As he spoke, the fisherfolk began to hurl cooking pots, soup ladles, coconuts, mangoes, melons, chickens—whatever they had been able to lay hold of — at the enemy fleet. One tall fisherman, in his enthusiasm, took a whole pail of eels and threw it aboard the Admiral's flagship. Then the little fishing boats turned around and quickly sailed past the harbor, leaving the Admiral and his warships in full command of the river.

The Admiral chortled. "Did they really think they could conquer our mighty armada with coconuts?"

"It would seem they are a rather primitive people, sir," said the Helmsman.

The Admiral surveyed the village and the castle. "No trouble here," he said smugly. "The fishing boats have disappeared behind a bend in the river. Not a living soul on the streets, except for a few scrawny chickens and goats. It's clear the natives are terrified." He looked down at the water. "The tide is going out, but there's still plenty of depth here in the middle of the river. We'll wait for low tide to make sure we can dock."

Settling comfortably into his deck chair, he said, "Tomorrow, first thing, we'll surround the palace, destroy the arsenal, seize the jewels, and behead the Princess."

"Princess?" said the Helmsman. "What makes you think it's a Princess?"

The Admiral snickered. "Only a girl would be silly enough to fight a great naval battle with fruits and vegetables." He spotted an eel at his feet and kicked it scornfully. "Even fish! Ridiculous!"

An hour later, a tremendous shout came from below deck. *"Shipping water!"*

"What's that supposed to mean?" barked the Admiral.

"It means there's a leak," said the Helmsman.

From all over the fleet came the cry, *"Shipping water! We're shipping water!"*

The Admiral dashed down to the hold. There an extraordinary sight greeted his eyes. What appeared to be the top of a tree was poking through the bottom of the ship! Even as the Admiral watched, the tree top was slowly coming upward. Then another tree . . . and another . . . and another. By Neptune, more than a dozen were coming through the bottom! And where the hull had splintered around the tree trunks, the water was seeping in, slowly but steadily.

"Start bailing and saw off those crazy trees," bawled the Admiral.

"Beg pardon sir," said the Helmsman, "but if you get rid of the trees, the water will rush through. The trees are like corks. Take away the corks, and we'll all drown in the onrushing waters."

"Never mind," said the Admiral testily. "Send a message to the fleet. *'All ships to continue bailing. All ships' captains to report to my cabin for a Council of War.'*"

Some two hours later, when the captains were all assembled aboard the Admiral's flagship, the Helmsman stuck his head in the cabin door. "Sorry to interrupt, sir, but the water is draining out of the ships."

"Naturally, you blockhead," said the Admiral. "The men are bailing."

"No, no," said the Helmsman. "It's happening all by itself."

"Ye gods and little fishes!" gasped the Admiral.

He strode out on deck, stumbled on a coconut, then stopped and stared goggle-eyed at the astounding spectacle. All around, his whole fleet was stuck up on tree poles!

Suddenly everything became clear to the Admiral. He had been trapped. These devilish fisherfolk had used the tide against him. They had put in poles at low tide. He had come in with his ships at high tide. Then, when the tide went out, he was left stuck up on the poles.

Now he could hear a muted roar of laughter from the farmers, fisherfolk, and children who crowded the riverbank and docks.

From around the bend, the little fishing boats reappeared and surrounded the fleet. At their head was a golden swan boat, flying a flag of truce under the royal standard. It sailed up alongside the Admiral's flagship.

"Ahoy," said a fisherman. "Ready to surrender?"

The Admiral looked down and shook his fist. "Never! You just wait till we come ashore."

The tall fisherman grinned. "If you're thinking of sending your men swimming or wading to shore, think again. Because any man found in the water will be whacked on the head with an oar."

"Who the devil are you?" thundered the Admiral.

"I'm a fisherman. In fact, I'm the best fisherman around. Because I sacrificed a whole pail of eels for the glory of the Tiny Kingdom, the Princess has bestowed on me the honor of taking you to shore to negotiate the terms of peace."

"Never!" said the Admiral. "I'll go down with my ship."

"Your ship isn't going to go down," said the fisherman. "It will stay stuck up there on the tree poles until the ebb and flow of the tide breaks the fleet to smithereens."

The Admiral sighed, climbed down, and settled gloomily into the stern of the Royal Swan Boat. The tall fisherman rowed him to shore.

After the Admiral had changed into dry socks, he was summoned to the Council Chamber to face Princess Mat Mat and her three advisers.

"What humiliation!" cried the Admiral. "To be defeated by a woman!" He glanced at the young princess. "Not even a woman. A slip of a girl." He drooped miserably. "What's the difference. I shall be beheaded."

"Certainly we will behead you," said the Elder.

"I would cut off his feet," said the Younger.

"In my opinion," said In-Between, "justice lies somewhere in the middle."

The Princess clucked her tongue in disapproval. "No," she said. "Revenge is not our way. We do not believe that those who have wronged us should be punished or humiliated beyond what is necessary."

"You are not going to behead me?" said the Admiral.

"Ugh," said the Princess. "How distasteful."

The Admiral was completely fogbound. "Your Highness, what *are* you going to do?"

"Simple," said the Princess. "I shall supply you with two guides to take you and your men through the harsh mountainous terrain that leads back to your country and your Emperor. I shall also provide you with a two-week supply of food and water, as well as five water buffalo to help carry your provisions." The Princess was thoughtful. "We would appreciate your returning the water buffalo."

The Admiral knelt down before the Princess and kissed her hand. "Be assured, your animals shall be returned." His voice trembled with gratitude and relief. "Your Highness, I shall never forget you, nor the kind and gentle ways of your kingdom." Tears filled his eyes, rolled down his cheeks and onto his medals. "If there is anything I can ever do for you . . ."

"As a matter of fact, there is," said the Princess coolly. "I would ask you not to make unkind remarks about women and girls—especially princesses."

That evening, from the Royal Balcony, Princess Mat Mat and her three advisers watched the long winding caravan of enemy soldiers and sailors. At the front, leading his men, the Admiral, bedecked with medals and sniffling from a head cold, sat astride the fattest water buffalo. All along the road winding into the mountains, the farmers, fisherfolk, and children waved goodbye to them.

"It is good," said the Princess to her advisers. "We won the battle, and since the Admiral is returning home with his men, he will not lose too much face with his Emperor." She sighed wistfully. "How close we came to celebrating One Hundred Years of Peace."

"Dear Princess," said the Elder, "what happened this morning could hardly be called a battle. The only casualty was a sailor who got bonged on the head with a mango. Surely we can forget one small incident in a hundred years of peace."

"For the first time," said the Younger, "the three of us are in agreement about the number of firecrackers, flares, torches, Bengal lights, petards, Roman candles, and pinwheels for the celebration. One thousand."

The Princess was jubilant.

Thus it came to pass that within the week the Tiny Kingdom celebrated One Hundred Years of Peace—well, almost—with the biggest Carnival and Fireworks Display in its history. Not one, not three, but *twelve* fantastic red dragons slithered and writhed across the night sky.

And of all the happy farmers, fisherfolk, and children in the Tiny Kingdom, not one was happier than Princess Mat Mat.

Charlotte Pomerantz was born in New York City, where she lives with her husband, Carl Marzani—a writer—and their two children. Her many books for children include The Downtown Fairy Godmother, The Mango Tooth *and* Albert. *She is also co-author of* Eureka! *a musical about Archimedes.* "The Princess and the Admiral" *won the Jane Addams Book Award for "its contribution to the dignity and equality of all."*

By Helen Parramore Twigg
Illustrations by Sanford Hoffman

In the middle of a large city, towering high on all sides with walls and windows, lined underfoot with concrete and cement, bound on every front with signs that told you where to go and lights that told you when to go, there lived a small girl, a smaller boy, and an even smaller dog, on the thirty-second floor of one of the tallest buildings. Twice a day, once in the morning and once in the afternoon, they put a leash on the small dog and the three of them rode the elevator down thirty-two stories to the street, where they walked five blocks up and five blocks back on the cement sidewalk. They watched the traffic on the busy concrete street and they read all the signs along the way.

CURB YOUR DOG said one, so they did.

DO NOT LITTER said another, so they didn't.

CROSS ON WALK ONLY said another, and they crossed in the exact center of the crosswalk.

DO NOT LOITER said one at the hotel, so they hurried by quickly.

NO SPITTING said one at the subway entrance, and they passed it by with their lips squeezed together in two straight lines.

NO PARKING said one near the corner, and they relaxed a little because, of course, they had nothing to park.

When they were five blocks from their own tall building, they would turn and go back the way they had come, doing and not doing everything again all the way home.

One afternoon, as they reached the place to turn and go back, the small girl, whose name was Lavernia, said to the smaller boy, whose name was Roosevelt, "Let's go a few more blocks."

"Oh, we shouldn't!" he replied.

"But we should!" she answered. "Look there!" She was pointing to a sign which said **THIS WAY→** .

The boy looked at it with distrust. "I never saw that there before." The small dog ran over to the signpost and smelled it very carefully, then she wagged her tail all the way up to her ears and barked excitedly.

"See?" said Lavernia. "Even Poppy wants to go. And dogs have a way of knowing things," she added wisely.

At that the boy agreed to go and the three started off going **THIS WAY→**

It really wasn't any different from the cement sidewalks of the blocks they had already walked along. Signs saying **SLOW—CHILDREN** made them slow down. Then the next one said **RESUME SAFE SPEED** so they walked faster. There were several signs bunched together at the corner with nothing but numbers on them. **101, 78, 63, 27A, 207.** These the children ignored because they weren't very good in arithmetic and they didn't know whether to add or subtract. Just beyond the numbers there was a sign which said **ONE WAY→** so they went that way until they came to one which said **STOP** .

"Gosh," said Roosevelt. "What do we do now?" He was uneasy about being so far from the places he knew.

"Well," replied Lavernia, "we have to look for another sign." They both looked up and down and right and left but they could see no more signs until Poppy began to bark and wag her tail. She was under a sign which said **PROCEED WITH CAUTION** so Roosevelt, Lavernia, and Poppy tiptoed cautiously for a whole city block. They tiptoed right up to a very fancy ironwork gate which blocked their way. They could go no farther.

They stood and looked it over carefully. The iron was shaped and fashioned into roses and leaves and twining vines. On one side there was a little sign which said **RING BELL—WALK IN** , and under it was a doorbell.

Roosevelt was afraid, but Lavernia rang the bell and together they pushed against the iron gate until it swung open, creaking and groaning dreadfully. They stepped through the opening very cautiously and stopped just inside. They were standing on a pebble path which led from the gate and disappeared behind a tree. All around the path was green, green grass, bright flowers, bushes, and tall, leafy trees. Sunlight shone down and made bright yellow splotches on the grass.

The children stood very still on the pebble path and looked around them with big eyes. Finally Roosevelt pulled her arm and said, almost whispering, "I never saw any place like this place . . ."

"Me neither," said Lavernia. "It doesn't sound like any place I ever heard, either . . ."

"And smell," added Roosevelt. "It even smells different."

They stood very close together with Poppy sitting very still at their feet sniffing and trembling. They looked and listened and smelled. They saw the green and gold of the plants and sunlight, and the bright colors of many flowers. They heard the buzzing of bees and the songs of birds, and the crunchy pebbles beneath their feet. They smelled the earth, the fragrance of flowers, and the green grass. They didn't know what to do or what to think.

"Lavernia," said Roosevelt, "there's no cement! No sidewalk!"

"Yeah," she answered, "and no tall walls of buildings, either!"

The boy moved even closer and held her hand. He was scared. "What are we going to do?"

"Don't be scared," she replied. "We'll just look for some signs. Look there, Roosevelt, there's one now!" Nearby under a bush there was a little sign, which Lavernia read: **PODOCARPUS** .

"What?" said Roosevelt. "Podocarpus? What's that mean?"

"I'm not exactly sure," she replied hesitantly. "Maybe we should find another one instead." So they looked for another while moving down the path a little and peering under the bushes.

"Aha!" cried Lavernia. "There's another!" And she read **SANSEVIERIA** .

"But what does it *mean?*" wailed Roosevelt, who was getting very worried about everything. Two tears slipped out of his eyes and slid down his cheeks.

Lavernia saw the tears and knew she had better give him a straight answer before he really started to cry. She said, very matter-of-factly, "It means 'take your shoes off.' " So they both did just that, and then, shoes in hand, they walked on the cool green grass, digging their toes into the damp earth. Poppy trotted along with them, her ears cocked and her tail up, sniffing and listening to everything.

Soon they spotted another sign by a curve in the path. Lavernia read **BROMELIA** and said surely, "We go this way now." She seemed to be so sure of herself that no one, especially a smaller boy, would have questioned her authority.

"Okay," he agreed, "but what does it mean?"

"It means a place to eat lunch," she answered without a moment's hesitation. She had begun to believe that she actually understood the signs.

"We don't have any lunch," said Roosevelt sadly.

"No, but we will have when we get to Bromelia's, you just wait and see."

"How do you know?" asked Roosevelt. "I bet you're just making up stuff to tell me so I won't cry. Besides, I am really hungry."

"I've got it all figured out," said Lavernia. Then she lowered her voice to a mysterious whisper and intoned slowly, "We are in a MAGIC PLACE and all the SIGNS-ARE-IN-MAGIC-LANGUAGE!" Her eyes were so wide and excited and her voice sounded so strange that Roosevelt believed every word she said. But he had to ask, "How come you can read MAGIC LANGUAGE and I can't?"

"Because I'm part of the magic," she answered with cool logic. "Now let's go eat lunch."

They ran down the path past several flowering bushes and many strange-leafed plants and arrived breathless in front of a lovely old gnarled tree covered with golden apples. They stared in disbelief and wonder, until Lavernia reached up and picked one for each of them. They threw themselves, tummies down, on the grass and ate the apples hungrily.

"You were right all the time," said Roosevelt, "and I thought you were just joking me. Gosh, you were even right about lunch. A real MAGIC PLACE for sure!"

"Of course," she replied.

Poppy began tugging at her leash so the children got up and followed her down the path until they saw a sign which said **EDELWEISS** . "That means 'Good-bye,' " said Lavernia, and sure enough, just beyond were the fancy ironwork gates where they had come in. They sat down and put their shoes on and together they pulled at the gates until they swung open. They went out, closing the gate carefully behind them, and they walked toward home, down the cement sidewalk between the tall buildings.

When they reached the corner, they turned to look back. They saw the ironwork gates with the roses and leaves and the bell, and then Lavernia saw something else. Over the gates was another sign, all worked in iron roses. She read **BOTANICAL GARDENS** .

"Does that mean MAGIC PLACE?" asked Roosevelt.

"Of course," she answered.

And so it was.

Helen Parramore Twigg is a professor of Interdisciplinary Humanities at Valencia Community College in Orlando, Florida.

Stories For Free Children

Peachy Pig

By Jane O'Reilly

Every summer Peter and his mother go to the country to visit Uncle John. They always plan to leave in June, right after the last day of school. Peter's mother makes lists of things to do, and then she makes lists of the lists, and then Peter has to help her check things off when they are done.

The lists look like this:

- Put away winter clothes.
- Finish writing magazine article before leaving.
- Take Peter to dentist.
- Clean apartment.
- Do not leave kitchen cupboards in a mess.

The note about the kitchen cupboards is usually written in by Peter's father, who can only come to the country on weekends. He says if he has to live alone all summer just because he works in an office in the city, he would rather live alone than with a family of cockroaches, and there will surely be cockroaches unless the cupboards are cleaned out first. Peter's mother says she can't possibly clean out the cupboards *and* finish writing her article. After a short argument, Peter's father agrees that he will have time to clean the kitchen himself on weekday evenings.

So Peter checks off "Finish writing article," and doesn't check "Clean kitchen cupboards." The dentist is on vacation by the time Peter's mother remembers to call for an appointment, so Peter checks off "Dentist," although it isn't exactly fair.

"Put away winter clothes" and "Clean apartment" are things Peter doesn't want to know about, but he helps a little and both jobs get done somehow, and he checks them off.

Peter likes the summer lists better than the lists they write in the city. City lists always seem to say things like "Do homework" and "Make bed." The summer lists say things like "Make raspberry jam," "Sleep late," and "Take long walks."

You can make good lists like that because Uncle John lives on the edge of a small town. Houses in small towns have lots of things left over from the old days, like horse barns, and garden plots, and brooks running under willow trees along the edge of the property, and Uncle John's house has all those things. Uncle John builds stone walls and fireplaces and new bathrooms for people. In the summer he takes things easy and helps Peter with the lists. When Peter arrives, Uncle John always asks to see the summer list, and then he adds things to it, and the things he adds are the best part of the summer.

This year, after supper on the first night in the country,

Uncle John carefully added:

- Ask Peter if he can lend a hand this summer.
- Chores: feed the pig and horse.

"Oh," said Peter, bursting with curiosity, "What pig? What horse?"

"Well, now," said Uncle John, "I bought a nice, gentle little pinto mare that stays down in the pasture under the apple tree. You and your mother might like to ride her."

Everyone forgot all about the fact that a pig was also mentioned on the list. Peter's mother was so excited she couldn't even wait until dessert was finished before she ran down to the pasture to see the horse. Peter's father hugged the horse while Uncle John told them all about her good points.

"What is her name?" asked Peter's mother.

"Tanya," said Uncle John. He didn't tell them it was his favorite name for a girl, even a girl horse, because it reminded him of a girl named Tanya he had known when he was very young and more romantic.

When they walked back from the pasture it was pretty dark out, and Uncle John switched on his flashlight. Just then, beyond the fence, Peter saw something move.

As far as Peter could see, it was brown and white and had a few black spots in the right places. It jumped in and out of the flashlight beam in a very independent way. Then, Peter remembered that Uncle John's list had mentioned a pig too.

"It looks like a pig, but nicer." said Peter.

"That's just what she is, a pig," said Uncle John. "I thought you should learn to raise your own supper."

"I don't think we should eat her yet," said Peter nervously. "She's too small." Secretly he doubted she would ever be big enough to eat.

When Peter went to bed that night, he took out a piece of paper and a pencil and he wrote his own list.

SUMMER, he printed in big letters across the top.

- Name the pig.

The next morning without realizing it, Peter's mother helped Peter check off that item fast. She looked at the pig and said: "Now *that* is an absolutely peachy pig!" Peachy *was* a peachy pig. Uncle John showed Peter how to feed Peachy. Slop the pig, he called it. They filled up a bucket with water, and they poured it in her trough with some pig mash. Peter was very surprised at her manners. She ate like a pig, with all four feet in the trough.

"You have to feed this pig before eight o'clock," said Uncle John. "She's a baby, and needs to have her meals early, and on time." After she ate she wanted to be scratched, so Peter climbed over the fence and gave her a good scratch, and Peachy rolled over like a pleased cat and grunted contently.

After only a week Peter knew everything about taking care of Peachy. She had her meals promptly at eight, twelve, and six. She especially liked waffles with maple syrup left over from Peter's breakfast.

When it was hot, Peter poured buckets of water into Peachy's pen, because a pig needs to roll in mud to cool off. The first time Peter made Peachy a puddle, she jumped in the air, squealed with delight, and then rolled and splashed and slithered until she looked like a great big mud ball.

Peter found out that pigs squeal terribly, especially when they are picked up. She makes it sound like I'm trying to murder her," Peter told his mother. "I was just teaching her to walk with a leash." It wasn't a very successful lesson. Peter wanted to go down to the store, and Peachy wanted to go into the pasture to see Tanya. Peter tried to carry Peachy to the store. Peachy squealed. Peachy won. They went to visit Tanya.

Peachy was very fond of Tanya, and she tried to arrange for them to be together. She dug a tunnel under her fence, disturbing all the grass, and most of the grapevine from under the pine tree.

"We'd better move that fool pig's pen before she starts uprooting the tree," said Uncle John, so they spent the afternoon hammering and digging and measuring, and by six o'clock Peachy had a new pen in the corner of the pasture. Tanya tried to get into the pen, right through the barbed-wire fence.

The only animal Peachy didn't like was Uncle John's faithless and stupid hen, who was spending the summer laying eggs and making nests and then wandering off and forgetting to sit on the eggs, and then starting all over again somewhere else. Uncle John was sick and tired of finding clutches of eggs underfoot every time he tried to saddle up Tanya, and one day he was so mad at the hen he decided to hypnotize her.

Uncle John held the hen's head down so that her beak was touching the barn floor. Then he took his finger and moved it in a straight line along the floor away from the hen's beak. "There now," said Uncle John. "She'll stay just like that until I move her." After about ten minutes Peter began to feel sorry for her, stuck as she was in that ridiculous position. He moved her gently with his foot, and she stood up, looking a bit bewildered and stalked off.

Throughout the summer, Peter's mother ignored all her lists, and forgot all her plans about getting lots of work done. She spent her time stewing up big vats of raspberry jam in the kitchen, and visting Tanya and taking walks.

One evening about suppertime, Peter's mother decided to feed Peachy herself. Peter and Uncle John were off somewhere, building a chimney, and Peachy was complaining. About an hour later, Peter came into the house calling for his grub. (Peter was pretty unbearable on the days he lent a hand, acting like a whole houseful of farmers.) No answer. It was very mysterious. The raspberries were burning on the stove, and there was no sign of Peter's mother.

Finally, they found her leaning against the fence of Peachy's pen. Peter shook her arm, and she seemed to wake up.

"What happened? she said, all confused. "I was standing here looking at the sunset, thinking about the mountains, and I was watching Peachy's tail, and . . . why, I think her tail hypnotized me, the way John hypnotized that chicken.

That night Peter wrote a postcard to his Aunt Harriet saying, "Peachy is hypnotizing," and Aunt Harriet had to call Peter's father and say, "Really, isn't Peter a little young to be hypnotized by a girl named Peachy?" and Peter's father had to explain who Peachy was.

Pretty soon, much too soon, it was almost the end of the summer, and Peter's mother began to make lists again.

- Find school shoes for Peter.
- Get kitchen cupboards cleaned before we go home.
- Call dentist.

Everything, from the middle of August until Labor Day, was always called "the last time" by Peter's mother, and she always said it with a sigh. "If we hate to leave so much," Peter said one night, "why do we have to leave at all?" And then his mother would say he didn't understand; real life was city life.

When Peter's mother came downstairs on one of the last mornings, of the last week, she found Peachy right in the middle of the kitchen, finishing off the last of the jars of raspberry jam. Peachy was a very pleased pig and Peter's mother was a very cross mother.

It may have been that morning that Uncle John began to talk about cabbage and ham, pork chops and sauerkraut, and spare ribs with French fried potatoes.

"Uncle John," said Peter, "we don't eat our friends."

"But, Peter," said Peter's mother several days later, "be reasonable. Uncle John can't keep feeding that pig all winter."

"Why can't we take the pig to New York?" asked Peter. "She could live in the pantry, and we could take her for walks in the park, and" Peter said, looking at his mother with a sly expression "we could write a book about our city pig."

So Peter's mother made a new list, on which she wrote, "Pack the pig." Uncle John said he had never heard of such foolishness, but he was glad they weren't going to take Tanya too. Peter's father said he had never heard of such foolishness, but did Peachy eat cockroaches by any chance, because someone had better because those kitchen cupboards were really beyond ordinary cleaning. Somehow they got Peachy into ther back seat of the car and started for home.

The drive back to the city was a nightmare. Peachy was perfectly well behaved, sitting up and taking an interest in the scenery, but people in the other cars couldn't believe their eyes, and kept swerving out of their lanes to get a closer look.

When they got to the city, the family tried to sneak into their apartment building, and Peachy made a terrible scene about getting into the elevator. The superintendent peeked out of her door to see who on earth was being murdered in the front hall, and Peter's mother smiled nicely and said, "Peter is always so tired after a long drive, he simply has tantrums."

Peachy seemed to find the pantry broom closet a very comfortable substitute for her barrel, and while she was interested in the cockroaches she showed no appetite for them. Instead Peter fed Peachy three cans of creamed corn, and they all went to bed.

At five the next morning Peachy began to grumble, and everyone jumped out of bed.

"It's the pig," said Peter, "she wants to go for a walk."

Peter's father decided to be the first to walk Peachy.

The afternoon papers reported that a man had been seen dressed in a raincoat and pajamas walking a pig in Central Park that morning at 5:15 A.M., and the people riding home on the subway reading their papers said: "Well, you just never know what will happen in New York."

Later Peter and his mother tried to walk Peachy down Broadway, and Peachy objected horribly when they tried to tie her leash to a parking meter in front of a butcher shop.

"I don't blame her," said Peter at dinner. "There was a ham in the window."

"Peter, dear," began his mother gently, "I don't really think this is going to work out."

"But you haven't written the book yet," said Peter.

Peter's father said something very rude about women writers whose careers involve keeping pigs in pantries, and Peter's mother said something rude about fathers who spend the entire summer without once cleaning out the kitchen cupboards. Then Peter's father said he couldn't take the stares and the crazy comments another day. That morning, in fact, someone had asked him if Peachy was a new breed of bulldog.

Somehow, they managed for a whole week. Peachy was very difficult but also very charming, and when people stopped and asked, "What is that?" Peter's father said, "That's my son's pig," and walked on very casually. He was getting quite fond of Peachy, although she was doing nothing about the cockroaches.

And then, on Monday morning, something happened. A man came to the door and delivered a very official-looking paper which said in no uncertain terms that Peter's family was being evicted from their apartment because they had broken New York City Housing Authority Code Rule ⊠1733 which forbids (it said large black type) the keeping of swine in dwellings.

Peachy, it seemed, was swine.

"We'll fight this thing every inch of the way, through the courts if we have to," said Peter's father.

"I am not going to be put out on the street because of a pig," said Peter's mother.

"Now we can go back and live at Uncle John's all the time," said Peter.

Instead, Peter's father called the Bide-a-Wee home and the American Society for the Prevention of Cruelty to Animals and the animal shelter, and they all told him they had no facilities for pigs. The animal shelter suggested a slaughterhouse in Brooklyn and this time Peter's father said, "We don't eat our friends."

"Wait a minute," he said. "I haven't been spending all that time in Central Park for nothing."And so he called up the Central Park Children's Zoo and offered them a pig that was used to the city, and children, and strange things to eat. And the zoo was delighted and said to bring Peachy right over.

The landlord refused to let them stay in his building, even though Peachy had moved out. He said he didn't want their kind of people in his apartment, the kind of people who would keep swine and still complain about cockroaches. So, after a great deal of trouble and making lists, Peter's mother found a new apartment where there were no cockroaches in the kitchen. And Peter wrote a thank you letter to Uncle John which said:

Dear Uncle John,

Thank you very much for the nice summer visit. Peachy has gone to live in Central Park and she loves popcorn. I wonder if next summer I could have some rabbits?

Love, Peter

And then he crossed "Thank Uncle John" off his winter list, and went to work on "Write pig book."

Jane O'Reilly's articles have appeared in "Time" magazine, "Ms.," "Vogue," "New York," "Atlantic Monthly," and other publications. She is also the author of "The Girl I Left Behind"

The Ten-Woman Bicycle

By Tricia Vita

Illustrations by Marion Crezee

Many years ago the new three-storied Horizon Bicycle Parts Factory was built beside a waterfall, seven-and-one-quarter miles away from the village of St. Vincent. As soon as the water began turning the waterwheel that set into motion all the machines needed to make bicycle parts, the manager began hiring villagers—or at least the *men* from the village—to operate the machines. The men were soon working as handlebar-benders, wheel-spinners, eyelet-punchers, pedalers, polishers, and tubers.

When several women tried to get jobs, the manager laughed and said, "Women can't ride bicycles, so how can you expect to work in a bicycle parts factory?" And so the women went home to cook and clean and sew, and watch their husbands and sons climb on shiny bicycles and ride to work in the morning.

After one year there was a great demand for bicycle parts and a great shortage of workers to make the parts. Whenever the factory manager sat down to think of a solution, he reluctantly came up with the same thought: Perhaps I could hire a few women from the village and train them to make bicycle parts. And that was how it happened that ten women from the village of St. Vincent were finally hired to work in the Horizon Bicycle Parts Factory.

The ten women did the same work as the men and they did it as well. But they had to get up at five o'clock in the morning to make breakfast for their families, wash the dishes, and leave at six o'clock for their two-hour walk to the factory. After working all day, the women returned home to cook and clean and sew, and when they finally went to bed they were quite exhausted.

One day the first woman began feeling sleepy while turning the crucial curve in a cow-horn handlebar. Then the second woman was overcome by drowsiness in the middle of fitting a tire with an inner tube. Soon the third and fourth women nodded over their respective bicycle wheels while punching eyelets in the hubs. One by one, the ten women rested their heads on the worktable among unriveted rivets, sprung springs, and horsehair half-stuffed into seats, and fell fast asleep.

"Wake up the women and tell them to come to my office," said the manager to the overseer.

And so the ten women filed into the manager's office.

"Why don't you take a few days off and get some rest?" he suggested.

The first woman thought the manager had found a convenient excuse to fire them, now that the days of the great demand for bicycle parts were over. "We're falling asleep on the job only because we have to leave our homes so early and walk two hours to work. If we could ride

bicycles like the men, we wouldn't be tired," the first woman explained.

The manager couldn't have looked more surprised. "In all of this land, a woman has never ridden a bicycle!" he exclaimed.

"But if we could learn to make bicycle parts, surely we can learn to ride!" the second woman said.

"Well, perhaps," the manager replied. "But no one in this village has ever seen a woman on a bicycle. It would be embarrassing for you."

"I won't mind the embarrassment," the third woman said. "If only I could catch up on my sleep and keep my job!"

"Riding a bicycle will take one third the time of walking to the factory," the fourth woman calculated.

The manager was convinced. He began writing up sales slips for ten bicycles. But the fifth woman suddenly turned to the others and said, "I have my doubts about these bicycles. Won't our skirts get tangled in the spokes? And how will we get on and off gracefully?"

The manager imagined himself getting a glimpse of the woman's legs as she struggled to get on a bicycle. "It will be no trouble at all," he assured her, smiling as he indicated where on the dotted lines the women were to sign the slips.

"No, wait a minute! She's right," the sixth woman warned the others. "In these dresses, getting one leg across the front tube will be like trying to jump a high hurdle. We need a bicycle built for women."

"Let's drop that horizontal front tube from the steering post to the pedal bracket," the seventh woman decided.

"Then mounting and dismounting will be easy enough," the eighth woman added.

"How about dress guards to fit over the front and rear wheels?" the ninth woman suggested.

"Then we can ride safely, even in these skirts," the tenth woman concluded.

The ten women were in total agreement about the kind of bicycle they needed.

The manager was of another opinion. "I have heard of a bicycle designed for society ladies who sit on it sidesaddle and pedal with one foot. If you want a ladies' bicycle, I will order ten of those new models."

"Won't we lose our balance?" the first woman wondered.

"No," the manager replied. "The handlebars are shortened on one side and lengthened on the other while the track of the rear wheel is set slightly to the right of the front wheel to make up for any imbalance."

"This ladies' bicycle sounds ridiculous. It must be slow and unwieldy," the second woman announced. "We have to be at work at the same time as men, and make bicycle parts at the same rate of production as men, and yet your bicycles won't let us ride as fast as men. We don't want a bicycle that puts us at a disadvantage."

"We won't ride a man's idea of a woman's bicycle," the third woman remarked. "If we have bicycles of our own design, we will ride as well as any man."

The manager accepted the women's challenge. At

least, he thought, it might prove entertaining to watch the women try to ride bicycles.

Two weeks later, ten bicycles arrived from the Horizon Bicycle Assembly Factory. They had been assembled according to the women's design. That Sunday morning, the ten women met to practice riding around the quiet factory.

And when the ten women rode their new bicycles back to St. Vincent that Sunday evening, everyone who saw them stopped and stared in astonishment.

The next morning, the women bicycled to the factory in exactly one third the time it usually took them to walk. They left work at five o'clock, and would have arrived home at twenty to six, but the men from the factory followed on their own bicycles and badgered the women all the way.

"Hey, sweetheart! Let's see some more petticoat!" one man teased as he pedaled alongside one of the women. Another man cut in front of the women's wheels, swerved left to right, and yelled, "I'll race you to the tavern, dearies!"

All evening, word spread throughout the village that women from the factory were riding bicycles. The next morning dozens of villagers lined the street and waited. As the ten women bicyclists came into view, a man stepped into the path of the first woman's bicycle and shouted, "Just toot your horn, honey, and I'll get out of the way!" Many of the village women laughed and several children waited in ambush with pockets full of rocks. Even the dogs trotted after the bicycles, barking and snapping at the women's heels. When the women passed through the marketplace, vendors pelted them with rotten vegetables. A well-aimed tomato splattered on the sixth woman's dress and she complained to the constable, who only shook his head and said, "There ought to be a law against women riding bicycles."

After that, the ten women pedaled through pastures and climbed steep hills to avoid the village main street. Because they had to take roundabout routes to the factory, the women had to leave their homes as early as when they used to walk. And once again they began to feel drowsy in the afternoon. But this time the women did not fall asleep. They called a meeting to talk over their problems.

"We used to walk to work together," the first woman remembered. "Then we designed our own bicycles and rode to work together."

"At first, I couldn't keep up with the rest of you," the second woman continued. "But whenever the tenth woman disappeared behind the slope of a hill and I thought I was forgotten, the first woman appeared on the next crest, waving to me to catch up."

"Riding our separate ways has only added to our problems," the third woman declared.

"Let's ride to work together again and if someone stops one of us—why, together we'll all wait!" the fourth woman said.

"And together, we'll all be late for work!" the fifth woman cried.

"We'll never get to the factory at all, you mean! That's a

risk unless we are really determined to stick together," the sixth woman said.

"Determination isn't all that counts. The crowd can still separate us," the seventh woman pointed out.

"If only our ten bicycles were joined together," the eighth woman sighed.

"A Ten-Woman Bicycle!" the ninth woman shouted.

The tenth woman began taking inventory. "Two wheels, ten gears, ten handlebars, ten seats, ten sets of pedals, one endless chain plus ten women equals . . . ten times as fast!"

"Hold on, not that fast," the first woman cautioned. "But fast enough so that the villagers won't know what went by!"

Once again the women sent blueprints and bicycle parts to the Horizon Bicycle Assembly Factory and one day a Ten-Woman Bicycle was delivered. It weighed one hundred and fifty pounds and could carry eight times its own weight. It was almost twenty-four feet long, with two wheels that were each thirty inches in diameter and with ten of almost everything else. The ten women climbed onto their new machine and pedaled in unison down the dirt path in front of the factory. The men who worked in the Horizon Bicycle Parts Factory were impressed at last by the women's ingenuity. They gathered outside the gate to see the Ten-Woman Bicycle start off on its course. "We're rooting for you!" they cheered. "You can do it."

And they did! When the Ten-Woman Bicycle sped through the village without stopping, one villager said that the street had been visited by a meteor. But the villagers were even more awestruck to learn that the blur on their

horizon had been a Ten-Woman Bicycle. Twice a day the ten women whizzed by. Every morning and every evening the villagers lined the main street to witness the split-second spectacle.

Ten-Woman Bicycles became numerous in provinces from A to Z. The ten women owned the Ten-Woman Bicycle Parts Factory and its sister company, the Ten-Woman Bicycle Assembly Factory. And all the women in the land rode happily ever after.

Tricia Vita writes, bicycles and lives in Manhattan. Marion Crezee illustrates, bicycles and lives in Amsterdam. Their book, The Ten-Woman Bicycle, *has been published by the women's presses Sara in Holland, Sheba in England and Rallaros in Sweden.*

ONE FULL MOON IN JUNE

STORIES FOR FREE CHILDREN

One evening while Jane Doe and her own spotted Small One were eating their dinner, Jane sighed out a long one.

"Oh Golly," she said.

Her Small One just kept grazing ahead.

"It's been quite a while since I've seen such a sight as this full moon come rising on a warm, soft June night."

The Small One kept eating—though she nodded her head.

"It makes me feel restless, you know what I mean? It makes me feel restless to see such a scene."

Her Small One kept eating though she stayed very lean.

"I sure wish I weren't staying home here tonight. I'd sure like a swim in that yellow moonlight," Jane wistfully said.

Finally Small one raised up her head. . . .

And with a little smile, she said, "So why don't you go off and play— I've been stuck with you *all* day. Who cares about that silly moon—I'd rather stay here with Old Raccoon"

"You would? Well, say that's great! I wouldn't stay out really late," a happy Jane yelped with delight. "Gee, I hope that coon comes by tonight."

Just as she spoke, the raccoon rumbled into sight.

In a moment it was all quite plain, as Raccoon said, "Oh sure," to Jane when asked if he would hang around with Small One.

"Sure, Jane," he said. "You go on now and paint the town."

"Bye, Mom. have fun," said Small One quietly.

So Jane went trotting off with glee.

Then Small One bowed her head way over. "I think I'll eat a little more of this fine clover," she said to Coon.

The next time that Raccoon looked over she was lying in the clover—her head on her knee. "Looks fast asleep to me," he whispered. "This job's even easier than I figured."

Meanwhile Jane Doe had paused in flight. "Now where shall I go, shall I swim tonight? I know—the Silent Pool will be just right!"

She moved on quickly through the woods, running as quietly as she could. From time to time she did a dance—she hopped, she leaped, she jumped, she pranced.

When she reached the pool, it was quite a sight, gleaming brightly in the pale moonlight.

BY LYNN ROGERS

ILLUSTRATED BY KATHERINE OSBORN

Standing beside it, a short brown bear was having a drink with the old gray mare.

"Welcome, gentle deer," they said. "It's been a long time since we've seen you. What kind of things have you been into?" the bear asked Jane as she struggled to recall his name.

"Oh, just the usual and a little more," Jane answered lightly. "That Small One keeps me going nightly, daily and on Sundays, too." Then she asked politely, "and how are you?"

"Why, I'm doing fine. As I just said to Madeline here,'Sure as my name's Billy Bear, I've found me one outstanding lair. You'll have to come up and see it sometime."

"I'll do that, Bill, I really will," Jane said with a grin, "but right now I sure feel like a swim is what I want."

"You'll like it a lot," said Madeline. "The water's fine. We've just come out—and it's not too cold and not too hot!"

Jane plunged right in and splashed around. The moon was shining on the ground and in the air and even on the short brown bear. Jane felt frisky, fine and free.

"That's a pleasant sight to see," said the mare.

"Yes," said the bear. "Sounds like dear Jane deserved a break. Well, see you, Mad. It's getting late."

Bill lumbered off and very soon, the old gray mare glanced up at the moon. "My, my he's right," she thought and she called to Jane, "Goodbye, my friend." Then she, too, disappeared in the night.

Jane waved goodbye, and made a splash. She thought to herself, "I'd better dash. I'm far from home and I can see that nice full moon will be gone in a flash. But, golly, it sure was fun to roam, to feel so frisky, fine and free. To be alone with only me."

With a shake she was dry, with a leap she was gone and before she knew it, she was right back home.

She woke up the coon and thanked him alot.

"Nothing to it,"he said,"that's a fine little tot."

"I know it," said Jane. "Without her, I'd feel might lonely. But sometimes it's fun to go off with me only and play in the moon.

"So call again soon," said the coon as he left.

"Don't worry, I will," whispered Jane as she lay down beside Small One in the sweet-smelling hay. "I'd best go to sleep, tomorrow comes soon."

And just as she spoke—away went the moon.

Lynn Rogers is a free-lance gardener and mother of three, living in San Francisco. She writes book reviews and columns on childrearing and vegetable raising for the Noe Valley Voice, *and has a weekly radio show, "Raising Bread and Roses: Gardening Tips for the Bay Area." She is a member of the Feminist Writers Guild.*

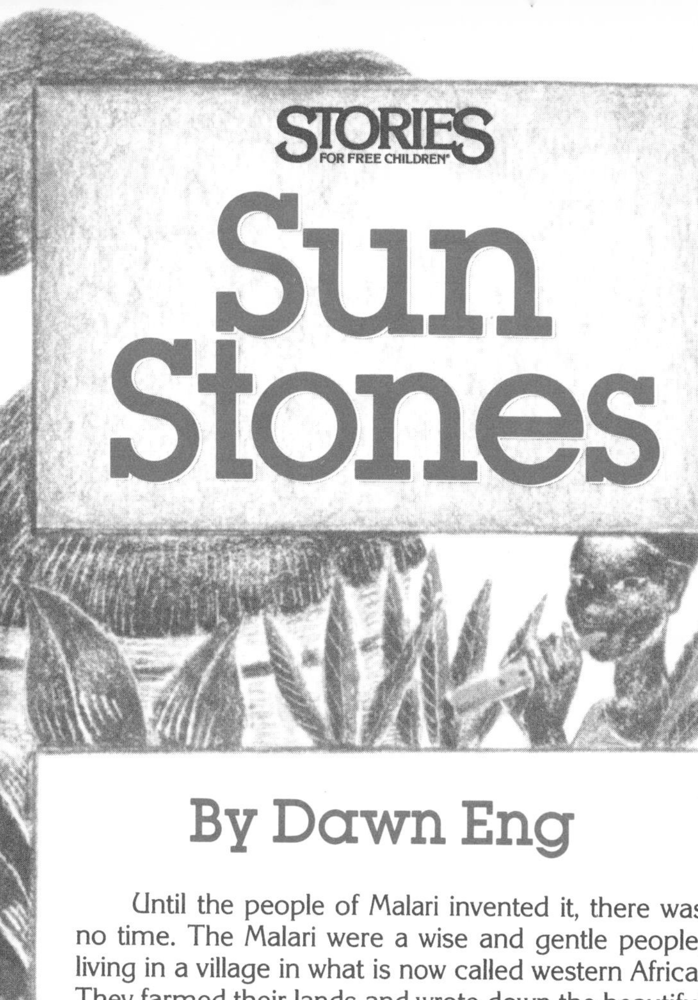

STORIES FOR FREE CHILDREN

Sun Stones

By Dawn Eng

Until the people of Malari invented it, there was no time. The Malari were a wise and gentle people, living in a village in what is now called western Africa. They farmed their lands and wrote down the beautiful music sung by birds in the forests around their farms. They were also great sculptors, forming trees, animals, and people by piling up different colored stones from the pebble quarry that was cared for by Luca's mother and father. And when they needed it, they invented time. Well, really, Luca discovered it, and that is how she earned adulthood. But now we are into our story.

Before there was time, the Malari didn't really miss it. No one got old, and no one followed a schedule. Babies were born and got bigger, they learned a lot of things, and they got wrinkled, and sometimes, when they were very wrinkled and very wise, they left their bodies behind and took all their learning back to the Great Wisdom to be born into other babies. They didn't need time for that. They had moon and sun, and when sun was there, people did their field work until it was finished, and then they played and wrote music and sculptured and hugged one another as much as they wanted to.

Sometimes the Malari had to decide things about life in their village, so all of the adults got

Illustrated by Julie Maas

together to talk about what to do. But of course being an adult had nothing to do with how many years old someone was. Without time, no one was ever eighteen or twenty-one, and besides, the Malari were much too wise to think being grown up happened for everyone exactly the same. Being adult meant being responsible and caring about the village and the other people in it. The Malari had a much better way of deciding who was grown up than our way of just counting years.

When a baby was born, the villagers planted a Kula tree, an important fruit tree for the community. The parents took care of the tree while the baby was still too little to walk, but after that, they taught the child to take care of its own tree. The villagers knew that some people took better care of their trees than others, so they grew better. When a child's Kula reached a height of four contor, everyone knew that it had been carefully tended, and its owner was ready to join in making decisions for the village. That is how the Malari became adults. Some children's little trees died because of neglect, and they had to start over with a new seed, but eventually every child became an adult, as soon as the Kula reached the right height.

Luca started caring for her tree when she could barely walk. She named it "Alia," which meant "light song," and she really loved it. She would watch it stretch and smile when the soft rains fell, and she would sit near it during sun, when she wasn't playing. She was careful to scrub its bark with leaves to keep bugs away, and she hardly ever forgot to water it between rains. Alia grew strong and beautiful along with Luca, and the child knew that she would soon be an adult. But one sun, something terrible happened. A storm blew up from the ocean and passed over the Malari village. This was not the gentle rain they knew, for it flooded down in a rage, and streaks of light fell from the clouds. After a while it was over, and everything seemed all right, until Luca went outside to visit Alia. And there it stood, split down the middle, looking and smelling like burnt firewood. Luca slipped down to the grass with her arms around the dead tree, and rains from her eyes ran down the split, but they could not make Alia grow.

Then Luca lost belief. It just wasn't fair! She had taken good care of Alia, but now it was dead. Luca's grandfather hugged her all through that sun, but it only helped a little. And not even her grandmother, who was the wisest, most wrinkled person she knew, could explain it in a way that made Luca feel better. She spent the suns sitting in the pebble quarry, not wanting to work or play or hug or even listen to birds, and she didn't want to plant a new seed. She watched the friends she used to play with all become adults as she sat on a log, just picking up stones and tossing them into piles without thinking about it. That is all she ever did during sun any more, toss stones into piles and feel sad and angry. But this is how Luca found time, though she wasn't looking for it.

One sun, Luca noticed that the piles she threw stones into were all about the same size during every sun. It seemed strange, because she wasn't trying to make them the same size. She counted several piles just to be sure, and every pile had between 720 and 730 stones in it. When sun came again, she counted out 720 stones, and when she had thrown them all into a pile, sure enough, sun was gone! Luca figured out that she could divide sun into parts by dividing up the stones into different-size piles, and she could always tell how much of sun was used up and how much was left, just by counting. Luca saw right away how important this was, and she ran home to tell her parents.

Her parents were very excited, especially her father, who loved to bake bread. Many Malari men and women liked to bake, but when they did, they couldn't take care of the fields or write down birdsongs or anything else, because they always had to watch the bread and cakes until they looked and smelled right, otherwise they would burn. But now all this was changed. Luca's mother lit the fire while her father mixed up his special bread dough and let it rise. He watched until it was high enough, while Luca threw stones into a pile. Then he put it into the oven and watched and sniffed until it looked and smelled just right. Again Luca threw stones into a pile. Later, when they all sat down to eat the bread and count the stones, they found that rising was about 125 stones, while baking was only about 70 stones.

Luca's mother hurried out to call a village meeting and tell the others about Luca's wonderful discovery. The villagers were grateful, and they voted that Luca was ready to be an adult for caring enough about the village to give them this helpful baking method. From then on, the Malari took turns tossing stones for baking, so everyone could do their farming and make sculptures and music and hug one another, and still bake good bread and cakes whenever they wanted to.

The Malari taught other villages about baking with sun stones, and they even asked birds to take messages across the ocean. So a lot of people heard about the stones, but some were silly about using them. They would sleep and work and even hug by the number of stones that were tossed; everything had to be measured in stones, and pretty soon the sun stones were ruining their lives. But of course the Malari were too wise for that. Sun stones were for baking, Kula trees were for showing who was grown up, and their work always got done. They remained great farmers, sculptors, and musicians, using sun stones only when they needed them.

The Malari word for stone was "tima," so you can see where our word "time" comes from. And even today, when we say a friend lives only a stone's throw away, we know it is very close—a place we can get to in very few sun stones.

Dawn Eng has been writing poetry for fifteen years, and has told stories for almost as long, but only recently began writing them down. She works as a translator of German technical documents for a patent law firm.

The Girl With The Incredible Feeling

Text and Illustrations
by Elizabeth Swados

A girl had an incredible feeling.

The feeling had no name, but it was very faithful and the girl treated it very well. The feeling made the girl act in incredible ways. It made her dance and sing wonderful songs. It made her laugh at things others fought over.

The feeling made nature enormous and wonderful.

She saw and heard incredible things. For instance: (1) men with grapes for beards, (2) beatnik basset hounds, (3) one friend who always talks and the other who always listens, (4) birds with sunglass eyes, (5) bank teller penguins, (6) baby adults, (7) a most unusual shoe, (8) a very curious hat.

One day a man came out of the shadows and complimented the girl on her feeling. He said there was great use for it all around the world. Thus began a series of unfortunate events. The feeling had to be dressed up and straightened out. Scholars, scientists, and politicians tried to explain it, and give it a name. People tried to steal the feeling and call it their own.

As the girl became more popular the feeling grew weak, faded from neglect, and finally disappeared.

At first the girl didn't notice it was gone, but soon she began to feel empty inside. She had horrible dreams. She could see right through herself. She couldn't feel anything. Everyone and everything looked and acted the same. The girl trusted no one. She knew she had to find her feeling.

The shadow man shouted after her, "Come back!" He tempted her with gifts. He told jokes to make her laugh and forget. She refused to listen and walked away.

Generous young people offered her their feelings. She refused politely and kept walking. She kept walking and walking.

Wise men offered amazing facts, but she ignored them and

kept walking. She kept walking and walking. . . . Until she was right back where she started. And then after a very long time beautiful smells, amazing sights and sounds—more incredible than before.

And although she was ashamed, she didn't have to apologize or explain. The feeling was hers again.

Elizabeth Swados is an author, composer and theater director whose works have appeared off and on Broadway and worldwide. Among them: "Nightclub Cantata," "Runaways," "Dispatches," "The Haggadah" and "Lullabye & Goodnight." She has published three children's books: The Girl with the Incredible Feeling, Sky Dance *and* Lullabye *(with Faith Hubley). Her first novel,* Leah and Lazar, *was published in 1982.*

Beautiful My Mane in the Wind

By Catherine Petroski
Illustrated by Karen Petroski

I am a horse, perhaps the last mustang.

This is my yard, this is my pasture. And I told her I hate her. My dam-mother. She does not understand horses. She doesn't even try. There are many things she doesn't notice about me.

Horses move their feet like this.

Horses throw their heads like this, when they are impatient, about to dash away to some shady tree. See how beautiful my mane in the wind.

Horses snort.

Horses whinny.

Horses hate her.

I am a girl horse. I am building a house under the loquat tree. It is taking me a long time.

My house is made of logs, logs that Daddy doesn't want. That is because our fireplace goes nowhere. It is just a little cave in the wall because this is Texas and it is mostly hot here. Our fireplace has a permanent fake log. I am six.

I will be six next month.

Anyway that is why I got the real logs when our weeping willow died and Mama pushed it over one Sunday afternoon. The bottom of the trunk was rotten and the tree just fell over and Mama laughed and the baby laughed and I didn't laugh. I hate her.

I hate also the baby who is a Bother boy.

Daddy cut the willow tree into pieces I could carry and gave them to me and now I am building a horsehouse under the loquat and waiting for a man horse to come along, which is the way it is supposed to happen.

I saw a picture of one and its name was Centaur.

Of a Sunday afternoon, in her stable

My room I also hate. Bother loves it best and squeals when he gets to its door, because he thinks it's nicer than his own room, nicer than the bigroom, nicer than anyplace at all. He likes best of all the blocks and the toy people. I build temples and bridges sometimes, but then he comes along. He throws blocks when he plays because he's just a baby. And a boy. And not a horse.

What I hate most about this room is picking up pieces of the lotto game when he throws it all over, picking up pieces of jigsaw puzzles that he has thrown all over. Wiping up the spilled water, picking up the blocks, the people. I hate his messes. I know that horses are not this messy. Mama says it is our fate to be left with the mess, but I don't think she likes it any more than I do.

She pays very little attention to me actually. She thinks I just read and I'm pretty sure she doesn't realize about the change. To a horse. She acts as though I'm still a girl. She doesn't observe closely.

Administering first aid to herself

The fact is there is a fossil in my hoof.

At school we have a hill that is called Fossilhill because there are a lot of fossils to be found there. Actually the fossils are very easy to find. You just pick up a handful of dirt and you come up with fossils. The trick is to find big fossils. I can always find the biggest fossils of anybody—snails and funny sea snakes and shells of all kinds.

The boys run up and down Fossilhill and don't look where they're going. It's no wonder they don't find many fossils. They come and pull Horse's mane. They scuff through where Horse is digging with her hoof. They sometimes try to capture Horse, since she is perhaps the last mustang and of great value. But mostly they are silly, these boys. They don't make much sense, just a mess.

Today I was trotting on the side of the hill and found the biggest fossil I have ever found in my life, which in Horse is I think twelve or maybe twenty-four years old. Then I found more and more fossils and other children came to the hill, even the girlygirls who never look for fossils because they always play games I don't know how to play—House and Shopping

and Bad Baby. But they tried to find fossils today and asked me if this was a fossil or that, and they found many, many fossils. And we all had a good time. And when we had found all the fossils we had time to find, our teacher said, Put them in your pockets, children, and if you don't have pockets put them in your socks. And we did, and that's why there is a fossil in my hoof.

Girlygirls *vs.* Boyannoys *vs.* Horse

In my kindergarten there is a girl whose name is Larch. It is a funny name for a girl. It might not be such a funny name for a horse, but Larch isn't a horse because she is in fact the girl leader because she decides what games are going to be played and will let the boys tie her up. And the other girls too. When they tie people up they don't use real rope because our teacher wouldn't allow that. If they tie me up with their pretend rope it doesn't work. They think I just don't want to play, but the truth is I'm a horse and stronger than a girl and can break their girlygirl rope.

It's more fun being a horse. More fun than being a girl too, because they just play Housekeeping Area and none of them really knows yet how to read even though they pretend to. I can tell because they can't get the hard words. So they don't let me play with them. My mother says it's all right because they wish they could enjoy stories themselves and next year they will all read and everything will be all right.

The reading is the real problem between the horse and the girls. I guess. But sometimes they do let me play with them, if they need a victim or a hostage or an offering.

Herself among the others

Horses are I think lucky. They do not seem to have friends, such as people, you know, for they do not seem to need friends. They have enemies—the snakes, the potholes, the cougars, the fancy-booted cowboys who don't know the difference between a canter and a hand gallop. What friends they have are on a very practical basis. Other horses with the same problems.

The wind.

A talk with herself

If I tell her what I am she will not believe me.

If I tell the others what I am they may rope me and tell me to pull their wagon.

If I tell a boy what I am he will invade my loquat house, and maybe it will be good and maybe it will be bad.

If I tell Daddy what I am he will act interested for a minute and then drink some beer and start reading again.

And if I tell Bother he will not understand even the words but will grab my mane and pull it until he has pulled some of it out.

What does it matter? What does it all matter? I will whinny and run away.

Who could blame me? Horses should not be abused, ignored, or made fun of.

Discussing the weather or nothing at all

Just a little while ago, when I needed to go out to race a bit and throw my head in the wind, she stopped me, my dam-mother, and asked me who I thought I was. A girl? A horse? My name? I know what she's thinking. The others at school ask me the same question.

So I said, a girl, because I know that's what I'm supposed to think. One thing I know, not a girlygirl, which would be stupid—playing games talking teasing being tied to the junglegym. I won't. Sometimes it's hard not telling her what I really think, what I know. That sometimes I'm a girl, sometimes I'm a horse. When there are girlthings to do, like read, which a horse never does, or go in the car to the stockshow or for ice cream or any of those things, I have to be a girl, but when there are hillsides of grass and forests with low-hanging boughs and secret stables in loquat trees, I am a horse.

Maybe someday there will be no changing back and forth and I will be stuck as a horse. Which will be all right with me. Because horses think good easy things, smooth green and windy things, without large people or Bothers or other kids at school, and they have enough grass to trot in forever and wind to throw their manes high to the sky and cool sweet stream water to drink, and clover.

Catherine Petroski, who lives in Durham, North Carolina, has published short fiction in literary magazines and in Ms. *Her books,* Gravity and Other Stories *and* Lady's Day, *will be followed by the book version of* Beautiful My Mane in the Wind, *to be published in 1983. Her daughter, Karen, illustrated this story at age thirteen.*

STORIES FOR FREE CHILDREN®

The Princess Who Stood On Her Own Two Feet

By Jeanne Desy

A long time ago in a kingdom by the sea there lived a Princess tall and bright as a sunflower. Whatever the royal tutors taught her, she mastered with ease. She could tally the royal treasure on her gold and silver abacus, and charm even the Wizard with her enchantments. In short, she had every gift but love, for in all the kingdom there was no suitable match for her.

So she played the zither and designed great tapestries and trained her finches to eat from her hand, for she had a way with animals.

Yet she was bored and lonely, as princesses often are, being a breed apart. Seeing her situation, the Wizard came to see her one day, a strange and elegant creature trotting along at his heels. The Princess clapped her hands in delight, for she loved anything odd.

"What is it?" she cried. The Wizard grimaced.

"Who knows?" he said. "It's supposed to be something enchanted. I got it through the mail." The Royal Wizard looked a little shamefaced. It was not the first time he had been taken in by mail-order promises.

"It won't turn into anything else," he explained. "It just is what it is."

"But what is it?"

"They call it a dog," the Wizard said. "An Afghan hound."

Since in this kingdom dogs had never been seen, the Princess was quite delighted. When she brushed the silky, golden dog, she secretly thought it looked rather like her, with its thin aristocratic features and delicate nose. Actually, the Wizard had thought so too, but you can never be sure what a Princess will take as an insult. In any case, the Princess and the dog became constant companions. It followed her on her morning rides and slept at the foot of her bed every night. When she talked, it watched her so attentively that she often thought it understood.

Still, a dog is a dog and not a Prince, and the Princess longed to marry. Often she sat at her window in the high tower, her embroidery idle in her aristocratic hands, and gazed down the road, dreaming of a handsome prince in flashing armor.

One summer day word came that the Prince of a neighboring kingdom wished to discuss an alliance. The royal maids confided that he was dashing and princely, and the Princess's heart leaped with joy. Eagerly she awaited the betrothal feast.

When the Prince entered the great banquet hall and cast his dark, romantic gaze upon her, the Princess nearly swooned in her chair. She sat shyly while everyone toasted the Prince and the golden Princess and peace forever between the two kingdoms. The dog watched quietly from its accustomed place at her feet.

After many leisurely courses, the great feast ended, and the troubadors began to play. The Prince and Princess listened to the lyrical songs honoring their love, and she let him hold her hand under the table—an act noted with triumphant approval by the King and Queen. The Princess was filled with happiness that such a man would love her.

At last the troubadors swung into a waltz, and it was time for the Prince and Princess to lead the dance. Her heart bursting with joy, the Princess rose to take his arm. But as she rose to her feet, a great shadow darkened the Prince's face, and he stared at her as if stricken.

"What is it?" she cried. But the Prince would not speak, and dashed from the hall.

For a long time the Princess studied her mirror that night, wondering what the Prince had seen.

"If you could talk," she said to the dog, "you could tell me, I know it," for the animal's eyes were bright and intelligent. "What did I do wrong?"

The dog, in fact, *could* talk; it's just that nobody had ever asked him anything before.

"You didn't do anything," he said. "It's your height."

"My height?" The Princess was more astonished by what the dog said than the fact that he said it. As an amateur wizard, she had heard of talking animals.

"But I am a Princess!" she wailed. "I'm supposed to be tall." For in her kingdom, all the royal family was tall, and the Princess the tallest of all, and she had thought that was the way things were supposed to be.

The dog privately marveled at her naiveté, and explained that in the world outside this kingdom, men liked to be taller than their wives.

"But why?" asked the Princess.

The dog struggled to explain. "They think if they're not, they can't . . . train falcons as well. Or something." Now that he thought for a moment, he didn't know either.

"It's my legs," she muttered. "When we were sitting down, everything was fine. It's these darn long legs." The dog cocked his head. He thought she had nice legs, and he was in a position to know. The Princess strode to the bell pull and summoned the Wizard.

Illustrated by Leslie Udry

"Okay," she said when he arrived. "I know the truth."

"Who told you?" the Wizard asked. Somebody was in for a bit of a stay in irons.

"The dog." The Wizard sighed. In fact, he had *known* the creature was enchanted.

"It's my height," she continued bitterly. The Wizard nodded. "I want you to make me shorter," she said. "A foot shorter, at least. Now."

Using all his persuasive powers, which were considerable, the Wizard explained to her that he could not possibly do that. "Fatter," he said, "yes. Thinner, yes. Turn you into a raven, maybe. But shorter, no. I cannot make you even an inch shorter, my dear."

The Princess was inconsolable.

Seeing her sorrow, the King sent his emissary to the neighboring kingdom with some very attractive offers. Finally the neighboring King and Queen agreed to persuade the Prince to give the match another chance. The Queen spoke to him grandly of chivalry and honor, and the King spoke to him privately of certain gambling debts.

In due course he arrived at the castle, where the Princess had taken to her canopied bed. They had a lovely romantic talk, with him at the bedside holding her hand, and the nobility, of course, standing respectfully at the foot of the bed, as such things are done. In truth, he found the Princess quite lovely when she was sitting or lying down.

"Come on," he said, "let's get some fresh air. We'll go riding." He had in mind a certain dragon in these parts, against whom he might display his talents. And so the Prince strode and the Princess slouched to the stables.

On a horse, as in a chair, the Princess was no taller than he, so they cantered along happily. Seeing an attractive hedge ahead, the Prince urged his mount into a gallop and sailed the hedge proudly. He turned to see her appreciation, only to find the Princess doing the same, and holding her seat quite gracefully. Truthfully, he felt like leaving again.

"Didn't anyone ever tell you," he said coldly, "that ladies ride sidesaddle?" Well, of course they had, but the Princess always thought that that was a silly, unbalanced position that took all the fun out of riding. Now she apologized prettily and swung her legs around.

At length the Prince hurdled another fence, even more dashingly than before, and turned to see the Princess attempting to do the same thing. But riding sidesaddle, she did not have a sure seat, and tumbled to the ground.

"Girls shouldn't jump," the Prince told the air, as he helped her up.

But on her feet, she was again a head taller than he. She saw the dim displeasure in his eyes. Then, with truly royal impulsiveness, she made a decision to sacrifice for love. She crumpled to the ground.

"My legs," she said. "I can't stand." The Prince swelled with pride, picked her up, and carried her back to the castle.

There the Royal Physician, the Wizard, and even the Witch examined her legs, with the nobility in attendance.

She was given infusions and teas and herbs and packs, but nothing worked. She simply could not stand.

"When there is nothing wrong but foolishness," the Witch muttered, "you can't fix it." And she left. She had no patience with lovesickness.

The Prince lingered on day after day, as a guest of the

King, while the Princess grew well and happy, although she did not stand. Carried to the window seat, she would sit happily and watch him stride around the room, describing his chivalric exploits, and she would sigh with contentment. The loss of the use of her legs seemed a small price to pay for such a man. The dog observed her without comment.

Since she was often idle now, the Princess practiced witty and amusing sayings. She meant only to please the Prince, but he turned on her after one particularly subtle and clever remark and said sharply, "Haven't you ever heard that women should be seen and not heard?"

The Princess sank into thought. She didn't quite understand the saying, but she sensed that it was somehow like her tallness. For just as he preferred her sitting, not standing, he seemed more pleased when she listened, and more remote when she talked.

The next day when the Prince came to her chambers he found the royal entourage gathered around her bed.

"What's the matter?" he asked. They told him the Princess could not speak, not for herbs or infusions or magic spells. And the Prince sat by the bed and held her hand and spoke to her gently, and she was given a slate to write her desires. All went well for several days. But the Prince was not a great reader, so she put the slate aside, and made conversation with only her eyes and her smile. The Prince told her daily how lovely she was, and then he occupied himself with princely pastimes. Much of the time her only companion was the dog.

One morning the Prince came to see her before he went hunting. His eyes fixed with disgust on the dog, who lay comfortably over her feet.

"Really," the Prince said, "sometimes you surprise me." He went to strike the dog from the bed, but the Princess stayed his hand. He looked at her in amazement.

That night the Princess lay sleepless in the moonlight, and at last, hearing the castle fall silent, and knowing that nobody would catch her talking, she whispered to the dog, "I don't know what I would do without you."

"You'd better get used to the idea," said the dog. "The Prince doesn't like me."

"He will never take you away." The Princess hugged the dog fiercely. The dog looked at her skeptically and gave a little doggy cough.

"He took everything else away," he said.

"No," she said. "I did that. I made myself . . . someone he could love."

"I love you, too," the dog said.

"Of course you do." She scratched his ears.

"And," said the dog, "I loved you *then.*" The Princess lay a long time thinking before she finally slept.

The next morning the Prince strode in more handsome and dashing than ever, although oddly enough, the Princess could have sworn he was getting shorter.

As he leaned down to kiss her, his smile disappeared. She frowned a question at him: What's the matter?

"You've still *got* that thing," he said, pointing to the dog. The Princess grabbed her slate.

"He is all I have," she wrote hastily. The lady-in-waiting read it to the Prince.

"You have *me,*" the Prince said, his chin high. "I believe you love that smelly thing more than you love me." He strode (he never walked any other way) to the door.

"I *was* going to talk to you about the wedding feast," he said, as he left. "But now, never mind!"

The Princess wept softly and copiously, and the dog licked a tear from her trembling hand.

"What does he *want?*" she asked the dog.

"Roast dog for the wedding feast, I'd imagine," he said. The Princess cried out in horror.

"Oh, not literally," the dog said. "But it follows." And he would say no more.

At last the Princess called the Wizard and wrote on her slate what the dog had said. The Wizard sighed. How awkward. Talking animals were always so frank. He hemmed and hawed until the Princess glared to remind him that Wizards are paid by royalty to advise and interpret—not to sigh.

"All right," he said at last. "Things always come in threes. Everything."

The Princess looked at him blankly.

"Wishes always come in threes," the Wizard said. "And sacrifices, too. So far, you've given up walking. You've given up speech. One more to go."

"Why does he want me to give up the dog?" she wrote.

The Wizard looked sorrowfully at her from under his bushy brows.

"Because you love it," he said.

"But that takes nothing from him!" she scribbled. The Wizard smiled, thinking that the same thing could be said of her height and her speech.

"If you could convince him of that, my dear," he said, "you would be more skilled in magic than I."

When he was gone, the Princess reached for her cards and cast her own fortune, muttering to herself. The dog watched bright-eyed as the wands of growth were covered by the swords of discord. When the ace of swords fell, the Princess gasped. The dog put a delicate paw on the card.

"You poor dumb thing," she said, for it is hard to think of a dog any other way, whether it talks or not. "You don't understand. That is death on a horse. Death to my love."

"His banner is the white rose," said the dog, looking at the card intently. "He is also rebirth." They heard the Prince's striding step outside the door.

"Quick," the Princess said. "Under the bed." The dog's large brown eyes spoke volumes, but he flattened and slid under the bed. And the Prince's visit was surprisingly jolly.

After some time the Prince looked around with imitation surprise. "Something's missing," he said. "I know. It's that creature of yours. You know, I think I was allergic to it. I feel much better now that it's gone." He thumped his chest to show how clear it was. The Princess grabbed her slate, wrote furiously, and thrust it at the Royal Physician.

" 'He loved me,' " the Royal Physician read aloud.

"Not as I love you," the Prince said earnestly. The Princess gestured impatiently for the reading to continue.

"That's not all she wrote," the Royal Physician said. "It says, 'The dog loved me *then.*' "

When everyone was gone, the dog crept out to find the Princess installed at her window seat thinking furiously.

"If I am to keep you," she said to him, "we shall have to disenchant you with the spells book." The dog smiled, or seemed to. She cast dice, she drew pentagrams, she crossed rowan twigs and chanted every incantation in the index. Nothing worked. The dog was still a dog, silken, elegant, and seeming to grin in the heat. Finally the

Princess clapped shut the last book and sank back.

"Nothing works," she said. "I don't know what we shall do. Meanwhile, when you hear anyone coming, hide in the cupboard or beneath the bed."

"You're putting off the inevitable," the dog told her sadly.

"I'll think of something," she said. But she couldn't.

At last it was the eve of her wedding day. While the rest of the castle buzzed with excitement, the Princess sat mute in her despair.

"I can't give you up and I can't take you!" she wailed. And the dog saw that she was feeling grave pain.

"Sometimes," the dog said, looking beyond her shoulder, "sometimes one must give up everything for love." The Princess's lip trembled and she looked away.

"What will I *do?*" she cried again. The dog did not answer. She turned toward him and then fell to her knees in shock, for the dog lay motionless on the floor. For hours she sat weeping at his side, holding his lifeless paw.

At last she went to her cupboard and took out her wedding dress, which was of the softest whitest velvet. She wrapped the dog in its folds and picked him up gently.

Through the halls of the castle the Princess walked, and the nobility and chambermaids and royal bishops stopped in their busy preparations to watch her, for the Princess had not walked now for many months. To their astonished faces she said, "I am going to bury the one who really loved me."

On the steps of the castle she met the Prince, who was just dismounting and calling out jovial hearty things to his companions. So surprised was he to see her walking that he lost his footing and tumbled to the ground. She paused briefly to look down at him, held the dog closer to her body, and walked on. The Prince got up and went after her.

"What's going on here?" he asked. "What are you doing? Isn't that your wedding dress?" She turned so he could see the dog's head where it nestled in her left arm.

"I thought you got rid of that thing weeks ago," the Prince said. It was difficult for him to find an emotion suitable to this complex situation. He tried feeling hurt.

"What you call 'this thing,' " the Princess said, "died to spare me pain. And I intend to bury him with honor." The Prince only half-heard her, for he was struck by another realization.

"You're talking!"

"Yes." She smiled.

Looking down at him, she said, "I'm talking. The better to tell you good-bye. So good-bye." And off she went. She could stride too, when she wanted to.

"Well, my dear," the Queen said that night, when the Princess appeared in the throne room. "You've made a proper mess of things. We have alliances to think of. I'm sure you're aware of the very complex negotiations you have quite ruined. Your duty as a Princess . . ."

"It is not necessarily my duty to sacrifice everything," the Princess interrupted. "And I have other duties: a Princess says what she thinks. A Princess stands on her own two feet. A Princess stands tall. And she does not betray those who love her." Her royal parents did not reply. But they seemed to ponder her words.

The Princess lay awake that night for many hours. She was tired from the day's exertions, for she let no other hand dig the dog's grave or fill it, but she could not sleep without the warm weight of the dog across her feet, and the sound of his gentle breathing. At last she put on her cloak and slippers and stole through the silent castle out to the gravesite. There she mused upon love, and what she had given for love, and what the dog had given.

"How foolish we are," she said aloud. "For a stupid Prince I let my wise companion die."

At last the Princess dried her tears on her hem and stirred herself to examine the white rose she had planted on the dog's grave. She watered it again with her little silver watering can. It looked as though it would live.

As she slipped to the castle through the ornamental gardens, she heard a quiet jingling near the gate. On the bridge there was silhouetted a horseman. The delicate silver bridles of his horse sparkled in the moonlight. She could see by his crested shield that he must be nobility, perhaps a Prince. Well, there was many an empty room in the castle tonight, with the wedding feast canceled and all the guests gone home. She approached the rider.

He was quite an attractive fellow, thin with silky golden hair. She smiled up at him, admiring his lean and elegant hand on the reins.

"Where have you come from?" she asked.

He looked puzzled. "Truthfully," he replied, "I can't remember. I know I have traveled a long dark road, but that is all I know." He gave an odd little cough.

The Princess looked past him, where the road was bright in the moonlight.

"I see," she said slowly. "And what is your banner?" For she could not quite decipher it waving above him. He moved it down. A white rose on a black background.

"Death," she breathed.

"No, no," he said, smiling. "Rebirth. And for that, a death is sometimes necessary." He dismounted and bent to kiss the Princess's hand. She breathed a tiny prayer as he straightened up, but it was not answered. Indeed, he was several inches shorter than she was. The Princess straightened her spine.

"It is a pleasure to look up to a proud and beautiful lady," the young Prince said, and his large brown eyes spoke volumes. The Princess blushed.

"We're still holding hands," she said foolishly. The elegant Prince smiled, and kept hold of her hand, and they went toward the castle.

In the shadows the Wizard watched them benignly until they were out of sight. Then he turned to the fluffy black cat at his feet.

"Well, Mirabelle," he said. "One never knows the ways of enchantments." The cat left off from licking one shoulder for a moment and regarded him, but said nothing. Mirabelle never had been much of a conversationalist.

"Ah, well," the Wizard said. "I gather from all this—I shall make a note—that sometimes one must sacrifice for love."

Mirabelle looked intently at the Wizard. "On the other hand," the cat said at last, "sometimes one must *refuse* to sacrifice."

"Worth saying," said the Wizard approvingly. "And true. True." And then, because he had a weakness for talking animals, he took Mirabelle home for an extra dish of cream.

Jeanne Desy is a free-lance writer living in Columbus, Ohio.

By Toni Morrison in collaboration with Slade Morrison

Patty and Mickey and Liza Sue
Live in a big brown box.
It has carpets and curtains and beanbag chairs
And the door has three big locks.

Oh, it's pretty inside and the windows are wide
With shutters to keep out the day.
They have swings and slides and custom-made beds
And the doors only open one way.

Their parents visit on Wednesday night
And you should see the stuff they get:
Pizza and Lego and Bubble Yum
And a four-color TV set.
On Christmas day
They got a picture of the sky
And a butterfly under glass
An aquarium thing with plastic fish
Made so it would last.

Oh, sea gulls scream
And rabbits hop
And beavers chew trees when they need 'em.
But Patty and Mickey and Liza Sue—
Those kids can't handle their freedom.

Now Patty used to live with a two-way door
In a little white house quite near us.
But she had too much fun in school all day
And made the grown-ups nervous.
She talked in the library and sang in the class
Went four times to the toilet.
She ran through the halls and wouldn't play with dolls
And when we pledged to the flag, she'd spoil it.

So the teachers who loved her had a meeting one day
To try to find a cure.
They thought and talked and thought some more
Till finally they were sure.
"Oh, Patty," they said, "you're an awfully sweet girl
With a lot of potential inside you.

But you have to know how far to go
So the grown-up world can abide you.
Now the rules are listed on the walls,
So there's no need to repeat them.
We all agree, your parents and we,
That you just can't handle your freedom."

Patty sat still and, to avoid their eyes,
She lowered her little girl head.
But she heard their words and she felt their eyes,
And this is what she said:
"I fold my socks and I eat my beets
And on Saturday morning I change my sheets.
I lace my shoes and wash my neck,
And under my nails there's not a speck.
Even sparrows scream
And rabbits hop
And beavers chew trees when they need 'em.
I don't mean to be rude; I want to be nice,
But I'd like to hang on to my freedom.
I know you are smart and I know that you think
You are doing what is best for me.
But if freedom is handled just *your* way
Then it's not my freedom or free."

So they gave little Patty an understanding hug
And put her in a big brown box.
It has carpets and curtains and beanbag chairs
But the door has three big locks.

Oh, it's pretty inside and the windows are wide
With shutters to keep out the day.
She has swings and slides and a canopy bed
But the door only opens one way.
Her parents visit on Wednesday night
And you should see the stuff she gets:
Barbie and Pepsi and a Princess phone
And a Japanese stereo set.
On Easter she got brand new jeans
With Pumas and a Farrah Fawcett shirt,
Marzipan eggs and jelly beans
And a jar of genuine dirt.

Oh, parrots scream
And rabbits hop
And beavers chew trees when they need 'em
But Patty and Mickey and Liza Sue—
Those kids can't handle their freedom.

Now Mickey used to live on the eighteenth floor
With two elevators to serve us.
But he had too much fun in the streets all day
And made the grown-ups nervous.
He wrote his name on the mailbox lid
And sat on the super's Honda

Blair

He hollered in the hall, and played handball
Right where the sign said not ta.

So the tenants who loved him had a meeting one day
To try to find a cure.
They thought and talked and thought some more
Till finally they were sure.
"Oh, Mickey," they said, "you're an awfully nice kid
With a wonderful future before you.
But you have to know how far you can go
So the grown-up world can adore you.
Now the rules are listed on the elevator door
So there's no need to repeat them.
We all agree, your parents and we,
That you just can't handle your freedom."

Mickey sat still and avoided their eyes
By lowering his little boy head.
But he heard their words and felt their eyes
And this is what he said:
"But I comb my hair and don't smoke hash
And every day I take out the trash.
I feed the hamster and water the plants
And once a week I hang up my pants.
If owls can scream
And rabbits hop
And beavers chew trees when they need 'em,
Why can't I be a kid like me
Who doesn't have to handle his freedom?
I know you are smart and I know that you think
You're doing what is best for me.
But if freedom is handled just *your* way
Then it's not my freedom or free."

So they gave little Mickey a knowing smile
And put him in a big brown box.
It has carpets and curtains and beanbag chairs
But the door has three big locks.
Oh, it's pretty inside and the windows are wide
With shutters to keep out the day.
He has swings and slides and a double bunk bed
But the door only opens one way.

His parents visit on Wednesday night
Just after the Merv Griffin show
With Blimpies and Frisbees and comic books
And matchbox cars that go.
For his birthday he got a Bakemaster's cake
And a poster of Jethro Tull
And a record that played exactly the sound
Made by a living sea gull.

Oh, baby seals scream
And rabbits hop
And beavers chew trees when they need 'em.
But Patty and Mickey and Liza Sue—
Poor kids—can't handle their freedom.

Now Liza lived in a little farmhouse
Where only the crickets disturbed us.
But she had too much fun in the fields all day
And made the grown-ups nervous.
She let the chickens keep their eggs;
Let squirrels into the fruit trees.
She took the bit from the horse's mouth
And fed honey to the bees.

So the neighbors who loved her had a meeting one day
To try and find a cure.
They thought and talked and thought some more
Till finally they were sure.
"Oh, Liza," they said, "you're a wonderful child
And we really don't want to remove you,
But you have to know how far to go
If you want grown-ups to approve you.
Now the rules are clear in everybody's mind
So there's no need to repeat them.
We all agree, your parents and we,
That you simply can't handle your freedom."

Liza sat still and avoided their eyes
By lowering her little girl head.
But she heard their words and felt their eyes
And this is what she said:
"But I've worn my braces for three years now
And gave up peanut brittle
And I do my fractions and bottle-feed
The lambs that are too little.
Will the crows not scream
And the rabbits not hop.
Won't the beavers chew trees when they need 'em,
If you shut me up and put me away
'Cause I can't handle my freedom?
I know you are smart and I know that you think
You are doing what is best for me.
But if freedom is handled just *your* way
Then it's not my freedom or free."

So they gave little Liza a pat on the cheek
And put her in a big brown box.
It has carpets and curtains and beanbag chairs
But the door has three big locks.
Oh. it's pretty inside and the windows are wide
With shutters to keep out the day.
She has swings and slides and a Loft-craft bed
But the door only opens one way.

Her parents visit on Wednesday night
Right after their bingo game.
They bring popcorn and Cheezits and pick-up-sticks
And dolls that are already named.
For Thanksgiving she had her own stuffed duck
Prepared by a restaurant cook
And a movie camera all set up
With a film of a fresh running brook.

Oh, the porpoise screams
And the rabbits hop
And beavers chew trees when they need 'em
But Patty and Mickey and Liza Sue—

Toni Morrison is the author of Song of Solomon *and* Tar Baby. *Slade Morrison was born in 1965. He lives in Rockland County with his mother and brother.*

THREE STRONG WOMEN

A Tall Tale from Japan

by Claus Stamm / Illustrated by Kazue Mizumura

Long ago, in Japan, there lived a famous wrestler, and he was on his way to the capital city to wrestle before the Emperor.

He strode down the road on legs thick as the trunks of small trees. He had been walking for seven hours and could, and probably would, walk for seven more without getting tired.

The wrestler hummed to himself, "Zun-zun-zun," in time with the long swing of his legs. Wind blew through his brown robe, and he wore no sword at his side. He felt proud that he needed no sword, even in the darkest and loneliest places. The icy air on his body only reminded him that few tailors would have been able to make expensive warm clothes for a man so broad and tall. He felt much as a wrestler should—strong, healthy, and rather conceited.

He thought: They call me Forever-Mountain because I am such a good strong wrestler—big, too. I'm a fine, brave man and far too modest ever to say so. . . .

Just then he saw a girl who must have come up from the river, for she steadied a bucket on her head.

Her hands on the bucket were small, and there was a dimple on each thumb, just below the knuckle. She was a round little girl with red cheeks and a nose like a friendly button. Her eyes looked as though she were thinking of ten thousand funny stories at once. She clambered up onto the road and walked ahead of the wrestler, jolly and bounceful.

"If I don't tickle that fat girl, I shall regret it all my life," said the wrestler under his breath. "She's sure to go 'squeak' and I shall laugh and laugh. If she drops her bucket, that will be even funnier—and I can always run and fill it again and even carry it home for her."

He tiptoed up and poked her lightly in the ribs with one huge finger.

"Kochokochokocho!" he said, a fine, ticklish sound in Japanese.

The girl gave a satisfying squeal, giggled, and brought one arm down so that the wrestler's hand was caught between it and her body.

"Ho-ho-ho! You've caught me! I can't move at all!" said the wrestler, laughing.

"I know," said the jolly girl.

He felt that it was very good-tempered of her to take a joke so well, and started to pull his hand free.

Somehow, he could not.

Claus Stamm lives in Japan.

He tried again, using a little more strength.

"Now, now—let me go, little girl," he said. "I am a very powerful man. If I pull too hard I might hurt you."

"Pull," said the girl. "I admire powerful men."

She began to walk, and though the wrestler tugged and pulled until his feet dug great furrows in the ground, he had to follow. She couldn't have paid him less attention if he had been a puppy—a small one.

Ten minutes later, still tugging while trudging helplessly after her, he was glad that the road was lonely and no one was there to see.

"Please let me go," he pleaded. "I am the famous wrestler Forever-Mountain. I must go and show my strength before the Emperor"—he burst out weeping from shame and confusion—"and you're hurting my hand!"

The girl steadied the bucket on her head with her free hand and dimpled sympathetically over her shoulder. "You poor, sweet little Forever-Mountain," she said. "Are you tired? Shall I carry you? I can leave the water here and come back for it later."

"I do not want you to carry me. I want you to let me go, and then I want to forget I ever saw you. What do you want with me?" moaned the pitiful wrestler.

"I only want to help you," said the girl, now pulling him steadily up and up a narrow mountain path. "Oh, I am sure you'll have no more trouble than anyone else when you come up against the other wrestlers. You'll win, or else you'll lose, and you won't be too badly hurt either way. But aren't you afraid you might meet a really *strong* man someday?"

Forever-Mountain stumbled. He was imagining being laughed at throughout Japan as "Hardly-Ever-Mountain."

She glanced back.

"You see? Tired already," she said. "I'll walk more slowly. Why don't you come along to my mother's house and let us make a strong man of you? The wrestling in the capital isn't due to begin for three months. I know, because Grandmother thought she'd go. You'd be spending all that time in bad company and wasting what little power you have."

"All right. Three months. I'll come along," said the wrestler. He felt he had nothing more to lose. Also, he feared that the girl might become angry if he refused, and place him in the top of a tree until he changed his mind.

"Fine," she said happily. "We are almost there."

She freed his hand. It had become red and a little swollen. "But if you break your promise and run off, I shall have to chase you and carry you back."

Soon they arrived in a small valley. A simple farmhouse with a thatched roof stood in the middle.

"Grandmother is at home, but she is an old lady and she's probably sleeping." The girl shaded her eyes with one hand. "But Mother should be bringing our cow back from the field—oh, there's Mother now!"

She waved. The woman coming around the corner of the house put down the cow she was carrying and waved back.

"Excuse me," she said, brushing some cow hair from her dress and dimpling, also like her daughter. "These mountain paths are full of stones. They hurt the cow's feet. And who is the nice young man you've brought, Maru-me?"

The girl explained. "And we have only three months!" she finished anxiously.

"Well, it's not long enough to do much, but it's not so short a time that we can't do something," said her mother, looking thoughtful. "But he does look terribly feeble. He'll need a lot of good things to eat. Maybe when he gets stronger he can help Grandmother with some of the easy work about the house."

"I'm coming!" came a creaky voice from inside the house, and a little old woman leaning on a stick and looking very sleepy tottered out of the door. As she came toward them she stumbled over the roots of a great oak tree.

"Heh! My eyes aren't what they used to be. That's the fourth time this month I've stumbled over that tree," she complained and, wrapping her skinny arms about its trunk, pulled it out of the ground.

"Oh, Grandmother! You should have let me pull it up for you," said Maru-me.

Her mother went to the tree, picked it up in her two hands, and threw it—clumsily and with a little gasp.

Up went the tree, sailing end over end, growing smaller and smaller as it flew. It landed with a faint crash far up the mountainside.

"Ah, how clumsy," she said. "I meant to throw it *over* the mountain."

The wrestler was not listening. He had very quietly fainted.

"Oh! We must put him to bed," said Maru-me.

"I hope we can do something for him. Here, let me carry him, he's light," said the grandmother. She slung him over her shoulder and carried him into the house, creaking along with her cane.

The next day they began the work of making Forever-Mountain over into what they thought a strong man should be. They gave him the simplest food to eat, and the toughest. Day by day they prepared his rice with less and less water, until no ordinary man could have chewed or digested it.

Every day he was made to do the work of five women, and every evening he wrestled with Grandmother. Maru-me and her mother agreed that Grandmother, being old and feeble, was the least likely to injure him accidentally. They hoped the exercise might be good for the old lady's rheumatism.

He grew stronger and stronger but was hardly aware of it. Grandmother could still throw him easily into the air—and catch him again—without ever changing her sweet old smile.

He quite forgot that outside this valley he was one of the greatest wrestlers in Japan and was called Forever-Mountain. His legs had been like logs; now they were like pillars.

Soon he could pull up a tree as well as the grandmother. He could even throw one—but only a small distance. One evening, near the end of his third month, he wrestled with Grandmother and held her down for half a minute.

"Heh-heh!" She chortled and got up, smiling with every wrinkle. "I would never have believed it!"

Maru-me squealed with joy and threw her arms around him—gently, for she was afraid of cracking his ribs.

"Very good, very good! What a strong man," said her mother, who had just come home from the fields, carrying, as usual, the cow. She put the cow down and patted the wrestler on the back.

They agreed that he was now ready to show some *real* strength before the Emperor.

"Take the cow along with you tomorrow when you go," said the mother. "Sell her and buy yourself a belt—a silken belt. Buy the fattest and heaviest one you can find. Wear it when you appear before the Emperor, as a souvenir from us."

"I wouldn't think of taking your only cow. You've already done too much for me. And you'll need her to plow the fields, won't you?"

They burst out laughing. Maru-me squealed, her mother roared. The grandmother cackled so hard and long that she choked and had to be pounded on the back.

"Oh, dear," said the mother, still laughing. "You didn't think we used our cow for anything like *work!* Why, Grandmother here is stronger than five cows!"

"The cow is our pet." Maru-me giggled. "She has lovely brown eyes."

"But it really gets tiresome having to carry her back and forth each day so that she has enough grass to eat," said her mother.

"Then you must let me give you all the prize money that I win," said Forever-Mountain.

"Oh, no! We wouldn't think of it!" said Maru-me. "Because we all like you too much to sell you anything. And it is not proper to accept gifts of money from strangers."

Next morning Forever-Mountain tied his hair up in the topknot that *all* Japanese wrestlers wear, and got ready to leave. He thanked Maru-me and her mother and bowed very low to the grandmother, since she was the oldest and had been a fine wrestling partner.

Then he picked up the cow in his arms and trudged up the mountain. When he reached the top, he slung the cow over one shoulder and waved good-bye to Maru-me.

At the first town he came to, Forever-Mountain sold the cow. She brought a good price because she was unusually fat from never having worked in her life. With the money, he bought the heaviest silken belt he could find.

When he reached the palace grounds, many of the other wrestlers were already there, sitting about, eating enormous bowls of rice, comparing one another's weight and telling stories. They paid little attention to Forever-Mountain, except to wonder why he had arrived so late this year. Some of them noticed that he had grown very quiet and took no part at all in their boasting.

All the ladies and gentlemen of the court were waiting in a special courtyard for the wrestling to begin.

Behind a screen sat the Emperor—by himself, because he was too noble for ordinary people to look at. He was a lonely old man with a kind, tired face. He hoped the wrestling would end quickly so that he could go to his room and write poems.

The first two wrestlers chosen to fight were Forever-Mountain and a wrestler who was said to have the biggest stomach in the country. He and Forever-Mountain both threw some salt into the ring. It was understood that this drove away evil spirits.

Then the other wrestler, moving his stomach somewhat out of the way, raised his foot and brought it down with

a fearful stamp. He glared fiercely at Forever-Mountain as if to say, "Now *you* stamp, you poor frightened man!"

Forever-Mountain raised his foot. He brought it down.

There was a sound like thunder, the earth shook, and the other wrestler bounced into the air and out of the ring, as gracefully as any soap bubble.

He picked himself up and bowed to the Emperor's screen.

"The earth-god is angry. Possibly there is something the matter with the salt," he said. "I do not think I shall wrestle this season." And he walked out, looking very suspiciously over one shoulder at Forever-Mountain.

Five other wrestlers then and there decided that they were not wrestling this season, either.

From then on, Forever-Mountain brought his foot down lightly. As each wrestler came into the ring, he picked him up very gently, carried him out, and placed him before the Emperor's screen, bowing most courteously every time.

The court ladies' eyebrows went up even higher. The gentlemen looked disturbed and a little afraid. They loved to see fierce, strong men tugging and grunting at each other, but Forever-Mountain was a little too much for them. Only the Emperor was happy behind his screen, for now, with the wrestling over so quickly, he would have that much more time to write his poems. He ordered all the prize money handed over to Forever-Mountain.

"But," he said, "you had better not wrestle any more." He stuck a finger through his screen and waggled it at the other wrestlers, who were sitting on the ground weeping with disappointment like great fat babies.

Forever-Mountain promised not to wrestle any more. Everybody looked relieved. The wrestlers sitting on the ground almost smiled.

"I think I shall become a farmer," Forever-Mountain said, and left at once to go back to Maru-me.

Maru-me was waiting for him. When she saw him coming, she ran down the mountain, picked him up, together with the heavy bags of prize money, and carried him halfway up the mountainside. Then she giggled and put him down. The rest of the way she let him carry her.

Forever-Mountain kept his promise to the Emperor and never fought in public again. His name was forgotten in the capital. But up in the mountains, sometimes, the earth shakes and rumbles, and they say that is Forever-Mountain and Maru-me's grandmother practicing wrestling in the hidden valley.

WHAT IS A MAN?

Story and Pictures by Fernando Krahn

The word spread very quickly: Beware of man! Young Orestes didn't know what a man was and boldly left his cave to find out by himself.

Soon he saw
his friend Hippo
at the river
and ran to ask him
if he knew about man.
"Well,"
Hippo said with a yawn,
"the only thing
I know about him
is that
he walks on two feet."

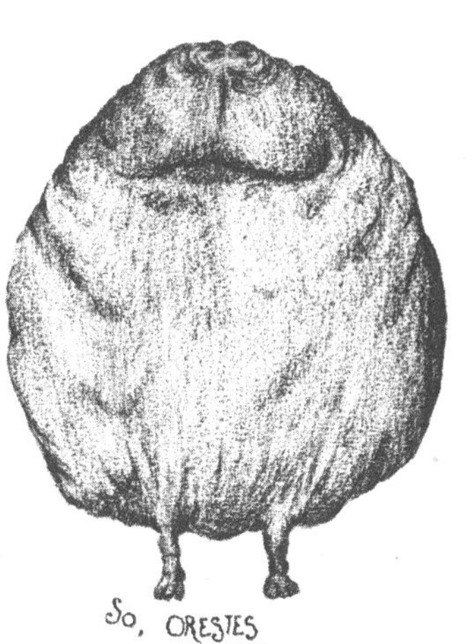

Orestes went
to see the giraffe.
"What is a man?"
he asked her.
"A man is someone with
a very short neck,"
answered the giraffe
with a sneer.

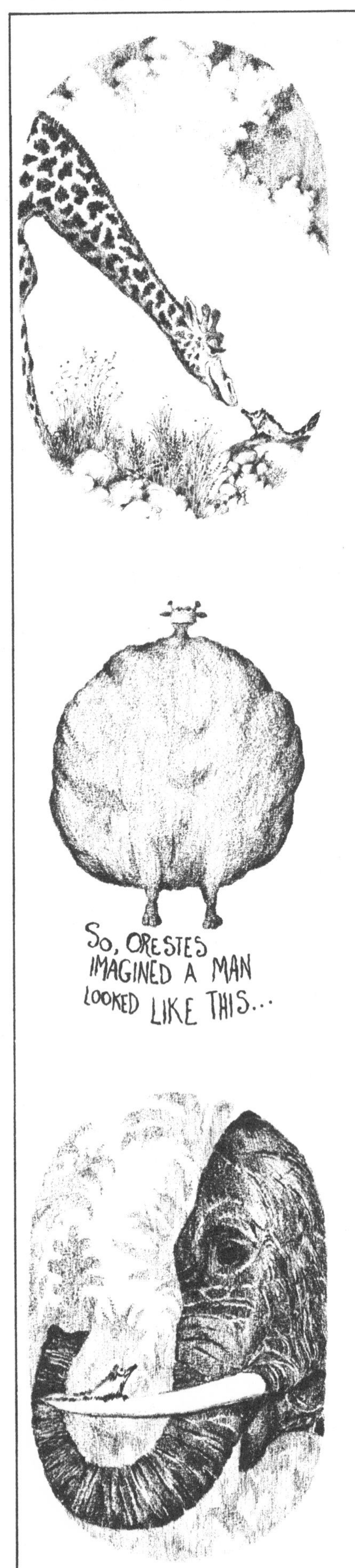

Out of the tall grass appeared an elephant. He told Orestes, "Man is just as wide and long as one of my legs and... what a silly little nose he has!"

Orestes approached the crocodile. "Man," he sobbed, "put my sister's skin around his waist. He calls it a belt."

Orestes met a peacock. "Man is a very envious creature," he said. "He comes in only dreary colors, so he pulls the multicolored feathers out of my tail to put on his head."

The leopard heartily agreed. "Man is someone who likes to dress himself in someone else's skin."

Orestes asked a monkey,
"What is a man?"
"That funny cousin of mine,"
was the answer,
"has short arms, no tail, and
his only visible hair
is on his head."

Orestes met a horse.
"I like man," said the horse.
"With his legs as long as his body,
he mounts on my back
and I take him for a ride."

The hog told Orestes:
"Man has a clear
and tender skin,
like a baby pig,
so he uses
the old hogs' skin
to make his shoes."

"Man is a curious being,"
said the hen.
"He has a soft
little beak
which he doesn't use too much."

"He cuts my wool
and knits a cloth of it. Shame!
I give him warmth
while I get chilled
out in the meadow."

"Do you know what a man is?"
Orestes asked a dog.
"Yes," said the dog,
"he is a good friend of mine.
He uses his two
long, warm arms to feed me
and caress me."

Finally
Orestes saw a real man.
He cautiously asked him:
"What is a man?"
The man answered:
"I couldn't tell you
how he looks because I am blind,
but I can tell you how good he can be
when he wants to."
So the blind man
took Orestes in his arms
and began to tell him
about the virtues of man.

As he listened Orestes fell asleep
thinking that...

A MAN IS
SOMEONE WHO
CAN LOVE

Fernando Krahn was born in Santiago, Chile, and now lives with his family in Sitges, Spain. He is a distinguished film maker and cartoonist, as well as illustrator and author of more than two dozen books for children.

Famous Women, Found Women

Part 2

THE SECRET SOLDIER

BY ANN McGOVERN

Deborah Sampson was only five years old when she had to leave her sick mother and her home in Plympton, Massachusetts. It was the year 1765, just 10 years before the start of the Revolutionary War.

She was sent to live with Miss Fuller, a relative of her mother's. For three years Deborah was happy. Then one day Miss Fuller became ill. Three days later she was dead. Deborah was now eight years old and without a home.

The only person who would take Deborah in was 82-year-old Mrs. Thatcher, who lived in Middleborough. Mrs. Thatcher was too feeble to do anything for herself. Deborah had to do everything. Sometimes Deborah thought she did not have a friend in all the world.

But the minister of Middleborough came to see how she was getting on.

He saw the feeble old lady nodding her head by the fire. He saw Deborah growing taller—and thinner—and paler. The good minister made a promise to himself. "I will get this child out of here," he said. He kept his promise.

A family! A laughing, loving, crying, hugging family! Deborah had almost forgotten what a family was. But the Thomas family was not *her* family. She knew what she was in the Thomas household. A servant. And she knew she would have to be a servant for eight years. That was the agreement. Deacon Thomas would give her a place to stay, food to eat, and clothes to wear.

There was plenty to do. She dressed the children, fed them, and told them stories. She helped with every job in the house and in the barn.

But the family was so lively and Deborah was kept so busy, she hardly had a moment to do what she liked best—reading.

In those days, people did not think it was important for girls to read. Some people thought too much reading gave girls brain fever.

Deborah begged Deacon Thomas to let her go to school sometimes. But there was so much work to do that she could rarely be spared. So Deborah borrowed the children's schoolbooks. At night, in her little room above the kitchen, she read until her candle flickered out.

At last Deborah was 18 years old. It was the year 1778 and she was free. But free to do what? She was a woman. That meant she could not learn a trade, the way young men did.

In the summertime she left the Thomas house. She—Deborah Sampson—who had never even been to school as a full-time pupil was going to teach in the town school. It was because of the war. Every man who could have taught in the summer school was busy with the war. There was no one left to teach.

There were a few girls in Deborah's class of 20 pupils. She remembered how she would have given almost anything to be able to go to school regularly and learn when she was young. So although she was supposed to teach the girls only sewing and knitting, and how to read a little, she taught them everything she knew. She taught them spelling and writing and things about the stars and the rivers and the mountains.

Deborah loved children, but she wanted to do other things—daring things—before she married and settled down. She dreamed of a great adventure. Doing housework from morning till night and looking after a houseful of babies was not her idea of a great adventure. Not yet. Not now.

Now she wanted to travel, to walk in different places, to see different faces.

In those days, if a poor man wanted to travel and have adventures, he joined the army.

"Why can't I join the army too?" Deborah thought. Then she laughed at herself.

"Me—Deborah Sampson—a soldier!" she thought. She knew the army was only for men.

"Wait," she told herself. "Why not me? Wasn't I a teacher without ever going to school? Wasn't I a *good* teacher? Why not a soldier? Why not dress like a man and be a soldier!"

That winter she worked as a weaver. She was weaving cloth, but she was also weaving plans. But she would need more money. She would have to get new clothes—men's clothes.

She would do one more weaving job. She wove cloth to tie around her chest so she would look flat-chested, like a boy. She wove a piece of cloth big enough to make a man's suit of clothes for herself. She bought a man's hat and shoes. One day she put on all the clothes for the first time and walked all the way to Boston.

On May 20, 1782, Deborah Sampson joined the army as a Continental soldier. She said her name was Robert Shurtleff.

"We'll put you down for three years, if the war lasts that long," she was told as she signed her strange name.

At first she was afraid to open her mouth to speak, afraid that she could not keep her voice deep enough. She was also afraid someone would find out she was a woman by the way she sat or walked or shook hands. But wonder of wonders—no one guessed who she really was! They thought she was young—15 years old—because she had no beard. Most of the men called her Bobby.

Her first test as a soldier was a hard one. She had to make a long march to West Point in New York.

She marched with 50 men. The march took almost two weeks. Every day she grew more and more tired, until she felt she could not go on. Every night she fell asleep in her clothes, like the rest of the soldiers.

One chilly, rainy afternoon the soldiers stopped to rest at a tavern. Deborah was warming herself at the fireplace. Suddenly she fainted and fell to the floor.

When she came to, her first thought was: "Have I been discovered?" Then she heard someone say, "What a pity such a young boy has to go to war."

Deborah breathed a sigh of relief. Her secret was still safe.

At West Point, she was given a uniform, a gun, and a heavy knapsack to carry on her back. She liked her uniform and the blue coat with its white buttons. She liked the new leather cap.

Every day she had to clean her gun and take part in the daily drill. She went on many raids against the Tories. (Tories were people who lived in America but who believed America should still be ruled by England.) Soon she stopped thinking of war as an adventure. War was the most horrible thing in the world, she thought. She heard the cries of men in pain. She saw them being shot down. She watched them die.

She had to go on long, long marches. Her shoes fell apart. Often she had to go without food for days. Sometimes she got so many blisters and sores on her hands she could hardly open or close her fingers.

But she never complained, and the other soldiers liked her for that. She did not drink or sing with the men, or take part in their wrestling contests or games. She tried to stay by herself as much as possible.

That winter, food was hard to get. The soldiers were always hungry. One day Deborah and a few soldiers rode their horses on a scouting party to a cave. The cave was filled with food that had been stolen by the Tories. The Tories had planned to give the food to the British soldiers.

There was honey in the cave and butter, bacon, and cheese. Deborah and the other soldiers were filling their sacks when the Tories discovered them.

Quickly Deborah got up on her horse and galloped away. The enemy was close behind, firing their guns. Suddenly she felt something warm and wet run down her neck. She touched her neck. Her hand came away bloody. Then she felt a sharp pain in her head. Deborah knew that she had been shot. She slid off her horse. All of her strength was gone.

She could hardly take a step and she could not stand alone. She looked down and saw that her boot was bloody. She had been shot in the leg too.

One of the soldiers stopped to help her. Deborah felt she would rather die than have him find out she was a woman.

"Leave me," she begged him. "Save yourself! I am going to die anyway!"

But the soldier took Deborah up on his horse and rode six miles to a hospital.

There the doctor gave her wine to drink and bound up her head with a bandage. He gave her extra medicine and more bandages for her neck in case she should need them later. Then he saw how pale she was and that she could hardly walk.

"Do you have any other wounds?" he asked, looking down at her boots.

"No," she said, her heart going like a cannon.

"Sit down, my young lad," said the doctor. "Your boot says you are lying."

Deborah knew she would have to act quickly. If he discovered she had been shot in the leg, he would make her take her clothes off so that he could remove the bullet. Then he would find out her secret.

"My head is throbbing with pain now," said Deborah. "Could I lie down for a while?"

The doctor led her to a small room. As soon as she was alone, she took out her pocketknife. She would use that knife and also the extra bandages and the medicine the doctor had given her. She had to take that bullet out of her leg herself.

The first time she tried, she could not do it. She tried again. The pain was more than she could bear. But if she left the bullet for the doctor to remove, he would find out her secret. The thought gave her courage to try once more.

This time, almost fainting from the pain, she dug out the bullet, and bandaged her throbbing leg.

She rested as long as she could, but it was not long enough. The strongest soldier with the same wound would have been sent home and would not have had to fight any longer.

No one knew how badly Deborah had been hurt. She didn't say a word to anyone. Her leg never healed properly. Two weeks after she had been shot, she was called to take part in a march. She started on the march. She was still weak and her leg throbbed with every step she took.

Richard Snow was another sick soldier. He was marching next to Deborah when he suddenly stumbled and fell to the ground. He could not go on.

Deborah thought fast. She told the officer in charge of the march that she would get Richard Snow to a nearby farmhouse. She said she would catch up with the others as soon as she could.

The officer agreed. This was Tory country. It was dangerous to stop and wait for one soldier to get better. The nearest house belonged to a farmer named Van Tassel. He was not very friendly, but he led them up to his cold attic. "It's good enough for rebels," he said.

Deborah's heart beat fast. "He must be a Tory," she thought, "or a friend of Tories."

He was. Every night he gave noisy parties for his Tory friends.

Deborah's leg was feeling stronger day by day, but Richard Snow was growing weaker and sicker. Deborah begged Van Tassel for a straw bed for the dying man.

"The floor is good enough for rebels," he said.

One day Deborah heard footsteps on the stairs. Her heart jumped, but the voice of a girl made her breathe easier. It was Van Tassel's daughter. She sneaked up food and water for Deborah and Richard.

But for Richard it was too late. On the tenth day, he died. Van Tassel's daughter helped Deborah bury him. Then Deborah set out to find the soldiers.

eneral John Paterson had heard of the quiet, brave soldier called Robert Shurtleff. On April 1, he chose Deborah to be his personal orderly. It was a high honor to serve him.

"I was given a good horse and fine equipment," she wrote. "I no longer slept on straw on the damp, cold ground, but on a good feather bed."

At last she could take off her dirty clothes and bathe in private.

In June she was sent to Philadelphia on an important mission. But it was not the time to be in the city. A terrible fever was spreading through Philadelphia. Many people got sick. Many died.

Deborah caught the fever too. One day she fainted and was put into a hospital bed. When she came to, she heard two men fighting over which of her clothes each one of them would take.

"Why, they think I'm dead!" Deborah thought in horror.

It took every bit of her strength to speak, to let the nurse know she was alive. The nurse rushed to tell the doctor that Robert Shurtleff in Bunk Five whom they thought had died was still alive. By the time Dr. Binney came, Deborah had sunk back into a coma. The doctor examined her and discovered her secret! Dr. Binney discovered that Robert Shurtleff, the young soldier, was really a young woman! But he never made a single sign that he knew.

He introduced Deborah as Robert Shurtleff to his wife and daughters. He told them about the brave soldier who had known so many adventures. She was invited to the fine houses of Philadelphia, still known only as a brave, Continental soldier.

September was a good time in Philadelphia. The peace treaty had finally been signed in Paris. All Philadelphia was celebrating the end of the war. November 3 was the date set for the soldiers to be sent home to their families.

Deborah grew stronger in Philadelphia. Soon she was well enough to travel. Dr. Binney gave her a letter to take back to General Paterson. When Deborah arrived at the camp in early October, she found General Paterson alone.

She handed him Dr. Binney's letter. She was so afraid of what Dr. Binney had written to the General that she ran out of the room before the General could say a word.

An hour later, General Paterson sent for her. Deborah was shaking like a leaf. He asked her to sit down. His voice was kind.

"Is it really true?" he said to her.

Her eyes filled with tears. For the first time as a soldier, she felt like sobbing and sobbing.

"What will be my fate, sir," she said, "if I say yes?"

"You have nothing to fear, Bobby—*er*, whoever you are," General Paterson said. "You have only my admiration and respect."

"Sir, I have no desire to hide the truth any longer," Deborah said. "I am who I am. Deborah Sampson and Robert Shurtleff. One and the same person."

She began to tell him all the names of the men in her company and about the adventures she had taken part in. She told why she had enlisted as a soldier and how she had kept her secret.

Deborah Sampson was discharged from the army in October, 1783. She had been in the army for about a year and a half. When she left she was given an excellent record of service.

Deborah returned to Sharon, Massachusetts, and that spring she met Benjamin Gannett, a farmer. Shortly after they met they were wed. It was almost three years from the day Deborah had signed up for the army.

Deborah Sampson Gannett who had been a soldier was now a farmer's wife. Her leg still hurt her. She could not do heavy work around the farm. Benjamin worked on the farm hard and well. They lived in a comfortable house. Roses and fruit trees flowered in the spring. A small stream flowed nearby.

It should have been a peaceful place for Deborah, after her many adventures. Still she longed to travel— to know what was beyond the next hill.

But they stayed in Sharon. They raised a family of three children—two girls and a boy. Then Deborah took in baby Susanna, whose mother had died. She raised Susanna as though she were her very own child. Deborah was a gentle mother. She had seen enough of war to know that she hated fighting. Deborah's children grew up to be peaceful and kind.

Deborah was 41 years old and still restless. Sometimes she taught in a school nearby. But that was not enough for her.

By then, her fame was well known. Her amazing story had begun to be told right after she got out of the army. Her adventures had been printed in the newspapers in New York and Massachusetts.

Everyone wanted to know about Deborah's life as Robert Shurtleff, the soldier. She gave her first talk in Sharon, her hometown. It was a big success.

She decided to give talks in other places—cities like Boston, Providence, New York. Ben did not stop her. But he would not go with her. He would stay home with the children and work on the farm.

Deborah Sampson was one of the first women in this country to travel alone and give talks for money. She made all the travel arrangements and took care of every detail by herself.

She put notices in the local papers.

Tickets may be had at the Courthouse from 5 o'clock till the performance begins. Price 25 cents, children half price.

She put on her old uniform and spoke against war. She told how she felt when she could not help the men around her who had been shot.

"I looked upon these scenes," she said, "as one looks on a drowning man—without being able to extend a hand."

She said she could not understand why men fought. "My young mind wanted to understand why man should rage against his fellowman, to butcher or to be butchered."

Some of the money she earned she sent home. "I hope my family makes good use of it," she wrote.

But she began to miss her family more and more.

"O dear, could I but once more see my dear children," she wrote in her diary. She was getting tired of traveling from one place to the next. Besides, her leg still hurt her, especially when she was tired.

The next year she came home for good.

Two years later, in 1805, the government voted to give a pension to the soldiers who had been wounded in the war. Deborah received her share.

Thirteen years later, the government gave her more money. She got $8 a month until she died on April 29, 1827.

More than a hundred years after she died, she was not forgotten. A warship was named after her.

Today in Sharon, Massachusetts; the house she lived in with Ben and her children still stands. In the quiet cemetery, a marble tablet has been put up in her honor. Nearby is Deborah Sampson Street, named for the daring young woman who looked for adventure—and found it.

Ann McGovern has written more than 35 books for children, among them Shark Lady: True Adventures of Eugenie Clark *and* The Underwater World of the Coral Reef, *which reflect her love of scuba-diving, the sea and its creatures. Her latest book is* Nicholas Bentley Stoningpot III.

STORIES FOR FREE CHILDREN®

Ride on, Sibyl Ludington!

By Ruth Eby

Historians agree that Sibyl Ludington did, in fact, ride many miles on the night of April 26, 1777, to muster the men in her father's regiment. This story is a fictionalized account of the many legends that have surrounded the event.

Spying on their neighbors was not exactly what Rebecca and Sibyl Ludington had in mind that April day in 1777 when they rode back to their homestead from a shopping trip to the general store in Fredericksburgh, New York. Both girls were astride Chestnut, their tawny yearling, when 16-year-old Sibyl spotted Redcoat horses in front of Neighbor Wellington's homestead. She suspected a plot was in the works to ambush her father, Colonel Henry Ludington, a patriot leader now attached to George Washington's staff in White Plains, New York. A reward of 300 guineas had been posted for his capture, dead or alive.

Many "sunshine patriots" had emerged since the signing of the Declaration of Independence the previous July. There was no way of knowing who could be trusted. After an hour of hiding behind a stone wall, the sisters had heard enough and seen enough to confirm Sibyl's suspicions. It was imperative that the sisters warn their father that their neighbors were actually meeting with the Tories, their enemy! Rebecca, her arms clasped around her sister's waist, held her breath as Sibyl goaded Chestnut to gallop home through the back trails.

When Sibyl was unsaddling Chestnut, she heard a noise in the loft of the barn. There she found Enoch Crosby, half-asleep, dressed as a shabby old peddler.

"Enoch Crosby! Have you given up soldiering and gone into business?"

He grinned and rearranged his pack, which overflowed with tinware, pewter, and pins. Since Enoch was an old family friend, Sibyl was surprised to find him in hiding. "This disguise is very effective," he explained. "It helps me slip in and out of British lines as an innocent tradesman."

Sibyl's eyes widened. "A spy?"

He nodded, lowered his voice to a whisper. "That is why I cannot accept Ludington hospitality at the front door. Too dangerous!"

A statue commemorating Sibyl's ride stands at Lake Gleneida in Carmel, New York.

Then Sibyl told Enoch about her own spying expedition.

"Young ladies should be quilting, not spying!" he exclaimed.

"We can't quilt our way to freedom!" she fired back, her eyes blazing.

Enoch was humbled. "Spoken like a patriot," he replied. He promised he would warn her father about the reward offered for his capture. He made Sibyl swear never to reveal his own identity and then slipped quietly into the dusk.

Sibyl knew Enoch had gotten the warning through, because when her father returned home in mid-April, he was accompanied by 20 men from his regiment. It was the Sabbath, forsythia was blossoming, and Abigail Ludington and her eight children gathered on the front veranda where the

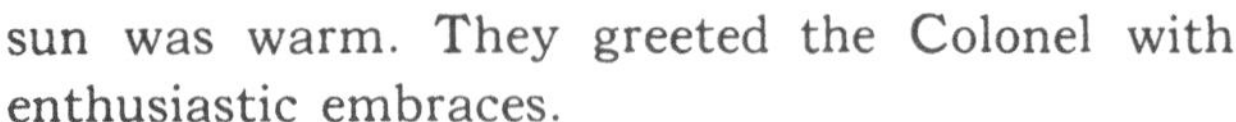

sun was warm. They greeted the Colonel with enthusiastic embraces.

Having safely escorted the Colonel home, the soldiers disbanded with orders to return to White Plains within a week. But a plan was conceived by the family to make it appear that a detachment of men still guarded the Colonel.

In the daytime Sibyl and Rebecca hid in the cornfields, disguised as patriot soldiers, on the lookout for any intruders. At night their mother sat by the upstairs window with a musket at her side while the others slept. Muskets and three-cornered hats were propped upon large casks that blocked the windows. At a given signal, the children were instructed to light candles in the rooms to give the illusion that soldiers hid in the shadows.

One evening, from the cornfields, Sibyl and Rebecca spied a figure darting behind the barn. Sibyl gave the signal: one large explosion from her musket. The household sprang into action! The children lit the candles, and the Colonel ran from window to window triggering the propped muskets, sending a barrage of lead balls out into the dark. The bounty hunter leaped upon his horse and galloped off, thankful that he had escaped the regiment of soldiers encamped at the Ludingtons.

Several days later a heavy rain beat down upon the tin roof. It was early evening, but the younger children were already asleep. Rebecca, who stood watch at the upstairs window, alerted them. "Horseman approaching!" The Colonel stood at the door, armed and waiting as the rider drew closer. The pounding hooves were coupled with Enoch Crosby's shouts: "Quickly, Colonel. I've important news!"

Enoch fell into the room, soaked, covered with mud, exhausted. The family waited as he warmed himself by the fire. When he could finally speak, he reported feebly: "Two thousand British troops have landed on the Connecticut coast at Compo. General Tryon is leading them. They're moving inland to Danbury!"

The Colonel grimaced. "Danbury? That's where we've stored our ammunition. Our supplies!"

Enoch could barely hold the tin cup of hot rum they offered him. "We're too late. By now Danbury must be a flaming torch."

Ludington smashed his fist against the wall. "We'll strike back. Enoch, you report to Generals Arnold and Wooster that we will furnish fresh troops."

Enoch, still shivering, responded: "I will, sir. But your men are scattered all over the countryside. You will have to send a messenger to recruit them."

"Yes, they must assemble here at dawn," the Colonel said, pacing, deliberating. He glanced at Sibyl. "If you were a boy," he mused, "I'd send you on this mission."

Sibyl chose her words carefully. "Is it less my revolution because I am a female? You have told me many times that I ride and handle a musket as well as you did at my age."

Her father argued: "My men live on rough roads in remote parts of Dutchess County. It would be dangerous even for any man to ride this night."

The girl would not be silenced. "There are no men to make the ride, and my brothers are too young. Besides, I know the back trails better than most. And your men would trust my call to arms."

After much consideration the Colonel relented. Sibyl was to recruit 38 men and have them assemble at the Ludingtons by dawn. She quickly threw on her cloak while her father listed the names and locations of the men she had to alert. Thrusting a musket and powder horn into the inside of the saddle, he advised her to "use it if you must." Her mother shuddered but offered no resistance to the plan. She knew what had to be done in their fight for freedom.

It's darker than the inside of a black cat,

thought Sibyl as she rode into the storm. She paced Chestnut at an even canter during the heaviest downpour and risked prodding him into a gallop only when she had a clear view of the terrain. Then at her urging he bounded forward in powerful leaps.

Heading south, she skirted the Fredericksburgh town square and reached the Cooper farm. She rapped on the door with a ferocity that matched the thunderstorm. "Captain Cooper! To arms! To arms!"

A lantern flickered at the window; then the door swung open, and Cooper appeared. He was tucking his shirtwaist into his breeches.

"Miss Sibyl? What's happened to bring you out this dreadful night?"

Sibyl gave her report. Cooper responded: "There are eight of us scattered in these hills. I'll alert them. You take the Main Post Road and head for the soldiers who live toward Carmel. You have a long ride ahead."

Sibyl nodded, resolutely. As she remounted, she heard him call after her. "Ride on, Sibyl Ludington! Good luck."

Cooper's confidence gave Sibyl new impetus. She was about to cut off the Main Post Road when out of the dreary mist appeared two drunken horsemen.

"Ho, there! A damsel in distress?" Both men tilted in the saddle, but somehow managed to stay aloft. The aroma of rum hung about them.

Sibyl reined up and demurely blinked her eyes, fluttering her wet lashes. "Please, kind sirs, I am on a mission of mercy seeking help for a household stricken with smallpox. No doubt I, too, will succumb to this dread disease." She loved her lie!

"Smallpox!" The word struck terror in their hearts.

Feigning great innocence, she asked, "Could either of you two gentlemen offer your services?"

Both of these "gentlemen" reversed their course and trotted off at such a pace that one of them failed to maneuver the turn in the road. He hung so far over the saddle that both he and the horse slid down the embankment, out of sight. Sibyl could not wait to share this tale with her family.

For the next few hours, at farmhouse after farmhouse, she was met with unwavering loyalty in response to her call to arms. Finally, though, the strain of riding took its toll. She had to rest. She tied Chestnut to a tree and stretched out on top of a large flat boulder. A fine mist still hovered. She took a swig of brandy from a flask her father had packed and felt the burning in her throat become a biting fire in her stomach. I'll make no wet bargain with the devil, she thought and put the flask away. She closed her eyes. Only one more patriot to alert, she thought. But, first, just a brief rest. As the brandy took effect, she dozed and then fell into a deep sleep. Sibyl never heard the rumble of hoofbeats; it was the raucous voices that awoke her.

"Captain Sitgreaves! A woman lies here. I think she's dead!" a British soldier shouted excitedly. Sibyl saw that she was surrounded by Redcoats!

"Here now, scoundrel, unhand me." Sibyl faced the young dragoon who shook her.

The commanding officer beckoned her to come down from her roost. Her reluctance was met with a nudge from the butt of a gun. She stood before the Redcoat captain, silently cursing herself for being caught.

The captain's ferret-eyes inspected her disdainfully. "Do you wish to explain yourself?"

What an arrogant prig, thought Sibyl. She suspected this officer would not believe her smallpox story. Thinking fast, she challenged him impudently. "Identify yourself, Captain!"

He was taken aback by her effrontery. How dare this impertinent child question him? "You are a prisoner of war, madam!"

Sibyl swallowed hard but unflinchingly matched his high-handedness. "I am on a mission of great importance!"

Impatiently he bellowed, "State it!"

"I've been sent to get help for General William Tryon. Two thousand British troops have landed at Compo, headed for Danbury, but they were ambushed by rebels at Fairfield!" She hoped she had muddled the facts enough to mislead him and send him off in the wrong direction.

The Captain was confounded. She had privileged information, this drenched slip of a girl. With new accord he asked, "Where have you come from?"

Regaining her composure, she borrowed her Tory neighbors' identity. "I'm a Wellington," she lied, "a loyal family if ever there was one. My brother was the courier for Tryon. He was mortally wounded but begged me to continue on his mission." She feigned sorrow (this was getting to be more fun!). "Please do not delay me. I must get through to Howe." (She had heard her father mention encounters with the Redcoat Howe.)

"You're too late. Howe has left for Brunswick! But we will alter our plans and head for Fairfield." He barked new orders to his men to "about face," then called down to Sibyl. "Return home, Miss Wellington. But take care. There may be rebels in the highlands."

Rebels under your nose! she thought, watching them speed away as she continued, to find the last recruit.

No one has adequately explained the several different spellings of Sibyl's name.

By daybreak, on April 27, 1777, a misty Sunday morn, 37 men arrived at the Ludingtons, each bearing stories of Sibyl's ride. But Sibyl herself had not yet appeared nor had Daniel Haines, the thirty-eighth recruit.

The Colonel's anxiety was apparent, but the troop could wait no longer. So 37 men and their commander mounted in a march to seek vengeance upon the British. At the bend, riding hard toward the house, the thirty-eighth man appeared in the mist. A cheer went up from the troops when Haines appeared. "Sibyl has done it!" they shouted.

As Haines saddled a fresh horse, he informed the Ludingtons that Sibyl was being held hostage by Jennifer Haines, his strong-willed wife. "Your daughter was so wet and weary, my missus wouldn't let her leave till she's fit. Young Sibyl wanted to ride back here with me. She sure gave us a battle, but my missus is a stone wall." He saluted the Colonel and fell into line with the troop. They rode off with a very proud father leading them.

EPILOGUE

On Sunday evening, at Redding, Connecticut, Ludington's men joined forces with the troops fighting under Generals Arnold, Wooster, and Silliman. On Monday morning the entire force encountered the British at Ridgefield, Connecticut, where they engaged in battle to avenge the sacking of Danbury. Although the patriots were short of ammunition and outnumbered, they were able to drive the Redcoats back to their ships at Compo. It was clearly a rout!

Alexander Hamilton wrote of this encounter to Gouverneur Morris: "I congratulate you on the Danbury expedition. . . . The spirit of the people on the occasion does them real honor [and] is a pleasing proof that they have lost nothing of that primitive zeal. . . ."

In celebrating the liberty won during the American Revolution, let us recall the bravery of the 16-year-old girl who rode undaunted on that dark and stormy night. "Ride on, Sibyl Ludington! Ride on!"

Ruth Eby has worked in radio and TV and has written musicals for children and organized seminars and festivals. One of her four children, Laura, helped in researching this story.

BIBLIOGRAPHY

Research at the historical societies in New York and Connecticut has supplied the author with documentation for the basic story. Other sources were:

Ludington-Saltus Records, Louis Effingham de Forest, A.M., ed., New Haven, Tuttle, Morehouse & Taylor Company, 1925.

Colonel Henry Ludington: A Memoir, Willis Fletcher Johnson. Printed by his grandchildren, L. E. Ludington & C. H. Ludington, New York, 1907.

A JOURNEY TO FREEDOM

By Gayle Pearson

Note: November 11th marks 100 years since the death of Lucretia Mott, a tireless fighter for women's rights. This story describes one of many experiences that affected her in a lifetime of struggle.

In 1840 a voyage from America to England was long and sometimes dangerous. But that didn't stop Lucretia Coffin Mott and her husband, James, who were on their way on the high seas to London to attend the first World's Anti-Slavery Convention in London.

At first Lucretia and James did not think they would be able to make the trip to England, even though Lucretia had been elected a delegate by the American Anti-Slavery Society. Her health was not very good that year. And a factory partly owned by James had been destroyed by fire, leaving them without much money. But several of their Quaker friends, who also hated slavery, gave the Motts some of their own money so that they could afford to go.

Also, Lucretia was able to save a little extra from the household money because she was so frugal. She never threw anything away! She saved scraps of cloth which she sewed together to make into rugs. She wrote on tiny pieces of paper, rather than waste them. How she found time to do all that, take care of her six children, be a faithful Quaker churchwoman, and tour the country speaking against slavery, no one knew.

Lucretia didn't stop working even on the voyage. While other passengers were resting, Lucretia was busy talking to people about slavery.

"You ought to take some time to relax, Lucretia," suggested James.

"I know I should," Lucretia answered. "But I have met several people on this ship who think that there is nothing wrong with owning another person. I must talk to them further. I'll rest in London," she said.

Most people in 1840 didn't see anything wrong with owning another person. Just as most people didn't think much about women not being able to vote.

Everyone thought of all kinds of reasons to defend slavery.

"We need the slaves to harvest the cotton and other products on farms and plantations," said the slave owners.

"It gives the Negroes something to do. They can't do anything else," others would say.

"The Bible says it's okay," even some ministers claimed.

And still others, ignorant of African history, said, "The Negroes have always been slaves!"

"You can't own someone just because the person's skin is black," Lucretia argued. But few listened.

Finally the ship reached Liverpool, England, where the journey to London continued by ferry, train, and horse-drawn carriage. When Lucretia and James reached their boardinghouse, Mark Moore's in Cheapside, they were exhausted.

Lucretia awoke the morning of the convention rested and eager to go to work with the other delegates to rid the world of slavery. She and James hurried through the crooked streets of London to Freemasons' Hall, where men and women from many countries had begun to gather. There they were surprised to find that a special place behind a barrier and curtain was being set aside just for women.

"This is a bad sign," Lucretia said to James. "It means that some of the leaders are going to try to keep us women from talking in the meeting, and from being able to vote."

This was not an unusual thing to do to women in 1840. Women weren't supposed to speak at meetings because it was thought to be "unladylike." They weren't allowed to do a lot of things that men could do. And, of course, they

Illustrated by Shelley Thornton

couldn't vote in elections.

"I can't believe this!" Lucretia whispered to a young, plumpish woman as she took her place behind the curtain. "Here we have worked so hard right alongside the men to fight slavery. We have come three thousand miles across the ocean. And we might not get to be part of this meeting! Just because we are women! It's not fair," she moaned.

The young woman, named Elizabeth, agreed with her, although she had not yet worked as hard in the antislavery movement. But she was only 20 years old and a new bride. Elizabeth smiled to herself when she realized that the woman seated beside her was Lucretia Mott. All the way across the Atlantic she had been warned by a fellow church member, James Birney, to keep away from this Mrs. Mott.

"She's a very dangerous woman," Mr. Birney had told Elizabeth. "Very dangerous. She does what she wants to do and pays little attention to how a woman ought to behave. She's not even a good Presbyterian like us."

Elizabeth had to put up with Mr. Birney as he paced the ship's deck spouting his opinions all the way across the Atlantic. And here she was, talking with Lucretia on the very first day! Why, the woman did not seem dangerous at all. She was quite small, with friendly brown eyes and a very kind face. One could hardly say that this slight figure in her long dark dress, cape, and bonnet was in the least bit fearsome.

Just then, one by one, the men at the meeting rose to give their opinions on whether or not the women should take part in the convention.

"I will not discuss the horrible subject of slavery in front of these fragile female beings," declared one man.

"The women have come three thousand miles and should be allowed to speak!" cried another.

"Absolutely not! The scriptures say women ought to keep quiet in public," said a third delegate, waving his Bible.

The men argued and argued until it was time to vote. When the votes were counted, the women had lost.

"This is a terrible day," Lucretia whispered to Elizabeth. "We came here to fight against slavery of a people—just because their skins are black. The convention has just voted against freedom for half of all humanity—whatever our race—just because we are women." Elizabeth saw Lucretia's face was lit with an angry fire.

At the end of the day Lucretia and Elizabeth walked arm-in-arm down Great Queen Street on the way back to their lodgings.

"I think," said Lucretia, "that we are going to have to begin to fight for our *own* rights. I can tell by what happened today that no one is going to do it for us."

"Yes," said Elizabeth, "but how can we get them to hear us?"

"I think that we must have our *own* convention," Lucretia said. "No one will be able to tell us we can't vote at our own convention!"

"A woman's convention! What a wonderful idea!" Elizabeth beamed. "When we get back to America we must keep in touch and begin making plans." She handed Lucretia a slip of paper on which she had written her address in America and her full name—Elizabeth Cady Stanton.

~

Lucretia still worked hard to rid the country of slavery, even though an angry, active woman was considered "unladylike." She worked just as hard for the freedom of women. She understood that the same sort of cruelty and inhumanity caused some people to think of other people as lesser forms of life whether they were women or blacks.

Eight years passed before Lucretia and Elizabeth were to meet again at the first Woman's Rights Convention in Seneca Falls, New York, the beginning of the battle for women's rights in America.

~

Gayle Pearson writes stories and plays for children and grownups. She lives in San Francisco.

~

AMELIA'S BLOOMERS

BY LINDA SCHECHET TUCKER

Elizabeth Smith Miller was working in her garden. She was not thinking about the weeds she was pulling out or the flowers she was transplanting. She was certainly not thinking about how nice her garden would look when the work was done. She was thinking about how awful she felt.

"I don't know why I continue to wear these horrid clothes when they make me so uncomfortable," she said to herself. Elizabeth was wearing long underwear trimmed with lace, a stiff petticoat that stood out like a bell, a flannel petticoat with a scalloped hem, another flannel petticoat, a plain white petticoat, a fancy white petticoat, and finally a huge skirt that went down to the ground.

Around her middle, under her dress, she wore stays, whalebone slats that were pulled in tight to make her waist look small. Over that she wore a camisole which protected her dress from the stays. Unfortunately, nothing protected Elizabeth's body from the stays, and her ribs hurt her where the stays were pressing against them. Elizabeth panted. It was hard for her to breathe in her tightly laced stays, and it was always difficult for her to stand up straight with the pieces of whalebone jabbing into her back.

This was Elizabeth's gardening outfit. In 1850, it was the outfit women wore all the time. They cooked in it, cleaned in it, and even took care of their babies in it. When they were at home, they didn't always pull their stays quite as tight as they did in public, and sometimes they took off one or two petticoats, but they always wore their long dresses. Elizabeth had just been married, and she was quickly learning how impossible it was to keep house in such cumbersome clothing.

Elizabeth was angry. "I simply cannot go on wearing clothes that I know are ridiculous. I don't care what the fashion is." She got up from her garden and went into the house. She went right to her sewing room and took out some fabric she had bought to make a new dress. She took out her pins, needle, thread, and scissors. Elizabeth was soon busily working. She was not making just another dress.

Earlier, Elizabeth had visited a rest home where women were recuperating from the effects of tightly laced stays. They had welts on their bodies and cracked ribs. Some of them even had hurt the inside parts of their bodies because of lacing the outside too tightly. Their waists had looked tiny, but their bodies were not healthy.

While they were recovering, the women wore special outfits given to them at the rest home. They wore loose-fitting pants that were tied closed at the ankle. Over the pants they wore dresses that did not go down to the floor but stopped about four inches below the knee. They were the first outfits Elizabeth had ever seen where you could actually tell that a women had legs.

The dresses were not pulled in at the waist, and, of course, the women wore no stays. These out-

Engravings from the Bettmann Archive

fits were called Turkish outfits because people in Turkey wore this style of pants. Elizabeth had decided to make herself a Turkish outfit.

The next morning Elizabeth came downstairs wearing her new clothes. Her pants were full and were gathered in with an elastic band at the ankle. Her dress was loose at the waist and reached a little below her knee. She wore no petticoats. Elizabeth felt comfortable. Her husband looked astonished. "Whatever are you wearing, Elizabeth?" he asked her.

"I'm sick and tired of wearing stays and petticoats. I don't see why I have to be uncomfortable all the time. This is my new outfit, and I don't care what you or anybody else thinks of it!"

"Just a minute, Elizabeth," he said. "In fact, I think your outfit is very sensible and looks much more comfortable than what you usually wear. I only asked you what it was."

Elizabeth was embarrassed that she had jumped down Charles's throat. Of course, she should have realized that he would approve of her new clothes. It was just that she was so worried about what people would say.

Elizabeth knew that her father would be very pleased when he saw her. He had often said that women would never win their rights until they started wearing clothes they could move in. When she was a child, Elizabeth had been the only girl in Peterboro, New York, who wore comfortable play clothes as the boys did. Her father had refused to dress her in long proper skirts.

Unfortunately, Elizabeth's neighbors did not find her outfit as sensible as her husband and father did. They could not believe that Elizabeth would walk out of her house in such clothes. Mrs. Williams in her stays and petticoats and long dress said to Mrs. Johnson in her stays and petticoats and long dress, "Have you seen Mrs. Miller?"

"I have indeed," said Mrs. Johnson to Mrs. Williams as their skirts dragged through the mud. "Imagine a woman wearing pants. Who does she think she is—a man?"

But Elizabeth continued to wear her Turkish outfit. She had worn the fashionable clothes long enough. Now she was determined to be comfortable. She made herself more Turkish outfits and began to wear them every day. She wore them at home and, despite disapproving glares of her neighbors, wore them into town as well.

It wasn't long after Elizabeth began wearing her new clothes that she decided to pay a visit to Elizabeth Cady Stanton. Besides being cousins, the two Elizabeths had been friends for many years. Elizabeth was sure that Lizzie would approve of her Turkish outfit. They had both long agreed that women could never expect to be able to do all the things that men could do as long as they could hardly move in their stays and petticoats.

Elizabeth arrived at Lizzie's house in Seneca Falls wearing full Turkish pants, a short dress, and a Spanish cloak all made of black broadcloth. She also wore dark furs and a beaver hat with feathers. Lizzie was astonished.

"How wonderful!" she said. "You must feel so comfortable and free. I've never seen such an outfit."

"You should make yourself one, Lizzie," Elizabeth said. "I've never felt so good. Look at how I can move." Elizabeth twirled around to show her cousin her freedom, as well as to show her how the outfit looked from the back.

"Oh, I don't know if I could wear such clothes in Seneca Falls," answered Lizzie.

The two women walked toward the house together, one with a tight waist and long dress, the other walking more briskly with her loose waist and Turkish pants. As soon as they entered the house, Lizzie heard her baby crying upstairs. She gathered up her skirts and climbed the stairs. She came down a few minutes later holding little Theodore in one arm and her skirt and petticoats in the other. It was late in the day, and it was difficult to see on the stairway.

"Lizzie, you should carry a candle. You could fall and hurt yourself and your baby walking downstairs in the dark like that."

Lizzie laughed. "Now how am I going to do that?" One hand was busy with skirts and petticoats, and the other was busy with a baby. "I only have two hands."

Elizabeth took Theodore out of his mother's arms and picked up a candle with her free hand. She walked up the stairs quickly and easily. When she reached the landing, she turned and looked at Lizzie at the foot of the stairs. "It's really quite simple," she said.

Lizzie was convinced. The next day she sat down and made herself a Turkish outfit of black satin. The two women could now be seen walking through Seneca Falls together in their loose pants and short skirts. They had never enjoyed walking so much. The disapproving looks of Lizzie's neighbors did not bother them. With no long skirts to get in their way and no stays to hamper their breathing, the cousins could walk for miles.

One day they stopped at the post office. Amelia Bloomer, the postmaster's wife, was busily working in a room next to the post office. She was the publisher of a monthly newspaper called *The Lily*. Amelia claimed that *The Lily* was the first paper in the United States that was owned, edited, and published by a woman. When Lizzie and Elizabeth arrived at the post office, Amelia was wrapping and addressing her newspapers for mailing. She had already written many of the articles for the new issue, edited the articles that other people had written, and arranged for the paper to be printed.

Just by coincidence, in this issue of *The Lily*, Amelia had written an article on how much women needed more comfortable clothing than the stays and petticoats that she was wearing. Imagine her surprise when Lizzie and Elizabeth walked into the post office wearing their Turkish pants and short skirts!

"Amelia, I'd like you to meet my cousin, Elizabeth Smith Miller," said Lizzie. "Elizabeth, meet Amelia Bloomer."

"How do you do, Mrs. Miller?" said Amelia. "Excuse me for not bothering with pleasantries, but please tell me all about your outfit. It just happens that I have been writing in my newspaper about the need for a change in women's dress. I must describe your clothing in *The Lily*."

Elizabeth gladly told Amelia all about how she had come to wear the Turkish outfit. Amelia realized the time had come to put into practice what she had been writing about. At home that night, she made herself a Turkish outfit.

Now Mrs. Miller, Mrs. Stanton, and Mrs. Bloomer could all be seen walking through Seneca Falls breathing deeply and moving briskly. The town talked of nothing else. Young boys taunted them as they walked.

Heigh! ho!
Thro' sleet and snow,
Mrs. Bloomer's all the go.
Twenty tailors take the stitches,
Mrs. Stanton wears the breeches.
Heigh! ho!
The carrion crow.

Mrs. Stanton's own son, who was away at boarding school, wrote to his mother to ask her please not to visit him in her new clothes. She wrote back to him.

"Now suppose you and I were taking a long walk in the fields and I had on three long petticoats. Then suppose a bull should take after us, why you with your arms and legs free, could run like a shot, but I, alas, should fall a victim to my graceful flowing drapery. My

petticoats would be caught by the stumps and the briars, and what could I do at the fences? Then you in your agony, when you saw the bull gaining on me, would say, 'Oh, I wish Mother could use her legs as I can.'

"Now why do you wish me to wear what is uncomfortable, inconvenient, and many times dangerous? I'll tell you why. You want me to be like other people. You do not like to have me laughed at. You must learn not to care for what foolish people say."

It was hard for a young boy to learn, but the three women truly did not care what foolish people said. They did what they wanted to do no matter who laughed at them.

Elizabeth went home to Peterboro and continued to wear her Turkish outfit in spite of her neighbors' stares and comments. Her husband, Charles, and her father always supported her decision to wear the new clothes. Elizabeth even wore her outfit to Washington, D.C., where her father was a Congressman.

Lizzie also continued to wear her Turkish outfit. She carried her baby safely and comfortably up and down the stairs in her house. She wore her new clothes all over New York State where she traveled to talk to people about rights for women.

And in the next issue of *The Lily*, Amelia wrote about the Turkish outfit and announced to her readers that she was now wearing it herself. Hundreds of women wrote to her asking for sewing patterns so that they could make their own Turkish outfits. But thousands of people were still shocked at the very idea of women wearing pants and short skirts.

Articles began to appear in other newspapers about the Turkish outfit. Most of them said that it was terrible for women to wear pants. Amelia wrote back to one newspaper saying, "If gentlemen really think they would be comfortable in long, heavy, skirts, well, let them wear them." More and more women began to wear Turkish outfits.

Since the other newspapers had first learned about the Turkish outfit from Mrs. Bloomer's articles, they called it "Mrs. Bloomer's outfit." Then they began to call it "the Bloomer outfit," and finally just "bloomers." The women who wore bloomers were called "bloomerites," and the whole idea of wearing the new clothes was called "bloomerism." Amelia insisted over and over again that it was Mrs. Miller who had first worn the outfit in public and that she should be given credit for her idea and her courage.

"They should be called 'millers,' not 'bloomers,' " said Amelia. But nobody listened. The name "bloomers" stuck. There was nothing that anybody could do about it.

Linda Schechet Tucker writes articles and textbooks and has a fondness for nineteenth-century literature. She lives in Hastings-on-Hudson, New York, with her husband and two children.

THE STRANGE VOYAGE OF NEPTUNE'S CAR

By Joe Lasker

On July 1, 1856, Joshua and Mary Patten set sail from New York on their second voyage around the world. As they sailed out of the harbor, Mary thought of the beginning of their first voyage almost two years before. How she had missed her mother and her home!

To fill time she had decided to learn all about the ship. Joshua taught her navigation: how to find where the ship was in the vast ocean, how to figure the direction it should sail, and how to find the distance it had sailed from one point to another. The voyage lasted a year and a half, and when it was over Mary was in love with ships and the sea.

Joshua Patten was Mary's husband and the captain of the great clipper ship, *Neptune's Car.*

The sailors called Joshua "The Old Man," and Mary "The Old Woman," even though Joshua was only 29 and Mary 19.

This voyage was a race. Two other clippers left New York the

same time as *Neptune's Car*, all steering the same course.

"It's fifteen thousand miles to San Francisco, and I hope we can win," said Joshua.

After several weeks at sea, the weather changed. Cold winds blew and a heavy snow fell. Joshua shook his head. "If the weather is so bad up here, what is it like down there at Cape Horn?"

The harsh weather made for hard work and mean tempers. Mr. Keeler, the first mate and a cruel man, beat and cursed the crew even more than usual. Mr. Hare, the second mate, the opposite of Mr. Keeler, was cheerful and helpful, even in bad weather, but he too worried about what lay ahead.

Mary could see that Mr. Keeler disliked her and the captain. She felt troubled. One night when Mr. Keeler was on watch, he fell asleep. The ship was endangered. A wind shift caused the sails to go loose and flap wildly, making a loud noise and changing the ship's direction. The noise, like the snapping of a whip, awoke Joshua and Mary.

Joshua dashed up on deck, and when he saw Keeler asleep he was furious. The wind could have torn the sails.

"Mr. Keeler, you endangered the ship and everyone on board!" Joshua shouted. "You set a terrible example for the crew just when we are nearing Cape Horn. I warn you, abandon your duty once more and you will be kept under arrest all the way to San Francisco!"

The first mate did not reply.

Awful! Awful! Joshua discovered Keeler sleeping on watch again and ordered him locked in his cabin, under arrest. Now Joshua had to add Mr. Keeler's duties to his own.

Ahead lay Cape Horn.

Howling winds and knife-edged sleet hit the ship, coating it in ice. Joshua was topside day and night, doing his own and the first mate's work, while Mary stayed below.

The captain caught what sleep he could, sitting in a chair lashed to the rail to keep from being washed overboard. Mary worried about him because he was always cold and wet. Even his food was icy and soaked by the time the steward could get it to him.

During a lull in the storm, Joshua joined Mary in the cabin. He was coughing and shivering with fever. She begged him to rest and to put Mr. Hare, the second mate, in charge until he felt better. Joshua refused.

Then Mary told him: "Joshua, before *Neptune's Car* returns to New York, you will be a father. I can't rest easy with you so sick, staying up on deck day and night. Please, get some rest."

Joshua touched her hand gently and said, "How wonderful that we are going to have a baby!" He sighed, "Get Mr. Hare."

When Joshua explained to the second mate why he was being given command of the ship, Mr. Hare answered: "Sir, I can handle the ship and the men all right. The problem is I don't know how to read or write or reckon." He pointed to the navigating instruments, maps, and logbooks on the table. Joshua looked at Mary, and they felt each other's helplessness and fear.

Driven by roaring winds, *Neptune's Car* reached Cape Horn. Mountainous waves thundered over the rail. Joshua, still sick, was up on deck.

At noon Mr. Hare burst into Mary's cabin carrying Joshua, who was unconscious. Mr. Hare had grabbed him just in time to save him from being swept overboard by a wave. As they put Joshua to bed, Mr. Hare said, "You will have to take over, ma'am!"

"What do you mean?"

"It's you or Keeler," answered Mr. Hare. "You two are the only ones left who can navigate, and nobody trusts Keeler. Take command! Make the captain comfortable. I'll see to the ship and crew and then report back to you for orders."

Mary knew he was right—she must save the ship. For the next two nights she did not sleep. She nursed Joshua and plotted the ship's course by "dead reckoning" through heavy fog, avoiding the rocky coast. Icebergs, like phantoms, loomed up unexpectedly. Somehow the ship kept going. Mr. Hare cheerfully followed Mary's commands. The ship groaned and shuddered from the pounding of the seas. Joshua shivered with fever. He could not see or hear.

The next day Mary and Mr. Hare were on deck. She shouted to be heard over the roar of the sea and wind. "The crew is so brave! Look how they risk death, climbing up the slippery, icy rigging in this blinding wind."

Mary and Mr. Hare watched as the sailors untied frozen knots and clawed at the ice-coated sails that weighed tons.

From that night on Mary decided she would sleep in her clothing to be ready for any emergency. Before daybreak, Mary was suddenly awakened and called up on deck. Three seamen, aloft on the wildly swaying topsail yard, had just been blown off into the sea.

"Lost! Lost!" Mary cried out. Already half the crew was helplessly sick. The ship will be crippled if we lose more men, she thought. What will I do then?

Again Mary got no sleep. There was too much to do. Waves, like walls of water, boarded the ship. *Neptune's Car* was soaked. The cook's fires were drenched: there was no hot food, no way to dry out their wet clothing.

Mr. Keeler sent Mary a note begging to be returned to duty and promising he would bring the ship safely to San Francisco. Mary tore it up angrily.

"Does he think I can forget how he put us all in danger?" she said. "He thinks I'm a fool because I'm a woman. But I know if he was ever in command he would take revenge on Joshua, who is sick and helpless. Let him stay where he is."

"We did it!" shouted Mr. Hare, bursting into the cabin. "Cape Horn couldn't stop us. We have just sailed into the Pacific Ocean."

Mary leaped to her feet. "We brought this gallant clipper around the Horn in eighteen days," she said to Mr. Hare. "I'm proud of the crew." They shook hands. The weather cleared briefly as if to celebrate, and sunlight danced on the water.

But there was still Mr. Keeler. He tried to stir up the crew to mutiny against Mary. He sent them messages. "Are you mad, letting a nineteen-year-old girl sail this clipper? She is bad luck! Three men died off Cape Horn. The captain is dying. Don't let her turn this ship into a coffin. Get rid of her!"

Mr. Hare advised Mary. "Trust the men. They don't want Keeler to be their captain. They remember how he beat them

and cursed them. They remember he endangered the ship by sleeping when he was on watch." Mary thought this advice was good, and she paid no further attention to Keeler.

Trade winds and the warm southern sun favored *Neptune's Car*. She raced along almost on her own, allowing Mary more time to nurse Joshua. Sometimes his sight and hearing returned to him for a while.

Working over her charts and maps one day, Mary saw that the ship was nearing California. Soon the strange voyage of *Neptune's Car* will be over, Mary thought. I'll miss this ship. I m proud to be its commander and proud that I navigated safely for eight thousand miles.

One morning *Neptune's Car* sailed into San Francisco Bay as crowds along the docks watched her come in. Mary could see the other captains studying her closely through long telescopes. She smiled. Their puzzled faces showed surprise that a woman was at the captain's post.

Before noon the sails came down and the clipper was snugged in at the dock. Joshua was rushed to the hospital. Two armed guards took Mr. Keeler to the city jail. Close friends met the ship and brought Mary to their home.

"For the past fifty nights I have slept in my clothing," she told them. "Tonight I hope to have a hot bath, and sleep in my comfortable nightgown, in a soft, dry bed. I hope Joshua will be all right." Then she sighed, "I'm so tired."

Joe Lasker is an artist and the writer-illustrator of many award-winning books for young people.

NEPTUNE'S CAR

DANIEL H. BEARSE, Commander,

Is now receiving Cargo at PIER 15 E. R., foot of Wall St.

This ship is now rendered famous for having performed her last voyage under the most trying circumstances; when, during the severe illness of her able commander, Capt. PATTEN, she was successfully commanded and navigated for **54 days** by his heroic wife, who, without the assistance of any officers, succeeded in taking the ship safely into the port of San Francisco; and yet, under all these circumstances, making a quick passage. It is only necessary further to refer shippers to the fact that this fine vessel has made the voyage to San Francisco in **105** and **97 days.** She insures at lowest rates. Dispatch as above may be relied upon. For Freight, apply to

WM. T. COLEMAN & CO., 88 Wall St.,

TONTINE BUILDING.

Agents at San Francisco, Messrs. WM. T. COLEMAN & CO.

In the race with the two other clippers, "Neptune's Car" finished second, reaching San Francisco on November 15, 1856, after a trip of four and a half months. Mary Patten is the only woman who ever commanded a clipper, and one of the very few women in history to command any large seagoing ship.

Captain Joshua Patten, blind and deaf, died in Massachusetts on July 25, 1857, four months after the birth of his son, Joshua, Jr. Mary Patten died on March 17, 1861, of an illness brought on by the rigors of the voyage. The hospital at the United States Merchant Marine Academy at King's Point in New York is named in her memory.

BY OPAL WHITELEY/EDITED BY JANE BOULTON

The Story of Opal

Her parents died before she was five. She was given to an Oregon couple whose own child had died, and they named her Opal Whiteley. Because her foster father was a lumberman, Opal spent her childhood in 19 different lumber camps, where she started writing this diary in the early 1900s. She was then about five or six. When Opal was 12, a foster sister discovered the diary in its hiding place and tore the pages into thousands of pieces. Opal stored the pitiful scraps in a secret box.

Desperately poor at the age of 20, she tried to sell a nature book she had written to Ellery Sedgwick, the editor of Atlantic Monthly Press. There was little in the book to "tempt a publisher," but the girl herself—"something very young and eager and fluttering, like a bird in a thicket"—had a special appeal. After hearing bits of her life story, Sedgwick asked if she had kept a diary of her interesting life. Opal burst into wordless tears. Then painfully, over nine months, she pieced together the shredded pages. In 1920, the diary was published as "The Story of Opal" in a limited edition of 650 copies.

Though the book is long out of print, Opal's story will never be outdated as long as we are touched by a lost and wondering child. Except for a few words that are charmingly misspelled, most of the spelling has been corrected. Since the words seemed like poetry, this is the form I gave them for this condensation. But the words are hers.

My mother and father are gone.
The man did say they went to Heaven
and do live with God,
but it is lonesome without them.

The mamma where I live
says I am a new sance.
I think it is something grown-ups
don't like to have around.
She sends me out to bring wood in.
Some days there is cream to be shaked
into butter.
Some days I sweep the floor.
The mamma has likes to have
her house nice and clean.

Under the steps lives a toad.
I call him Virgil.
Under the house live some mice.
They have such beautiful eyes.
I give them bread to eat.

I like this house we do live in
being at the edge of the near woods.
All the way from the other logging
camp
in the beautiful mountains
we came in a wagon.
Two horses were in front of us.
They walked in front of us all the way.

When first we were come
we did live with some people
in the ranch house that wasn't
builded yet.
After that we lived in a tent.
Often when it did rain, many
raindrops
came right through the tent.
They did fall in patters on the stove
and on the floor
and on the table.
Too, they did make the quilts
on the beds some damp,
but soon they got dried
hanging around the stove.

I found the near woods first day
I did go explores.
So many little people do live in them.
I do have conversations with them.

One way the road does go
to the house of the girl who has no
seeing.
When it gets to her house
it does make a bend
and it does go its way to the blue hills.
I tell her about the trees talking.
I tell her cloud ships are sailing
over the hills in a hurry.

Sometimes I read the books
that Angel Mother and Angel Father
did write in.
They tell me about all the great men.
Now I know what to name my
favorite mouse.
He is Felix Mendelssohn.

Today near eventime I did lead
the girl who has no seeing
a little way into the forest
where it was darkness and shadows
were.
I led her toward a shadow
that was coming our way.
It did touch her cheeks
with its velvety fingers.
And now she too does have likings
for shadows.
And her fear that was is gone.

Today is taking egg day.
I put my blue bonnet on
and take eggs to the folks all around.
I put Felix Mendelssohn in my pocket.
He does like to go for walks.
And sometimes he sleeps in my sleeve.
When he has wakeups
we try to find cheese.
He has likes for cheese.

New folks live by the mill.
Dear Love, her young husband does
call her.
They are so happy.
But they have been married seven
whole months
and haven't got a baby yet.
I pray prayers for Angels
to bring them one real soon.

When I told her, she smiled glad
smiles
and kissed me—two on the cheeks
and one on the nose.
Then I did have joy feels all over
and Felix Mendelssohn poked his nose
out of my sleeve.
She gave him a little pat
and I new Dear Love was my friend.

I decided to take the mother-pig for a
walk.
I went to the woodshed.
I got a piece of clothesline rope.
While I was making a halter for the
mother-pig
I took my Sunday-best hair ribbon—
and put the bow just over her ears.
That gave her the proper look.
When the mamma saw us go walking
by,
she took the bow from off the pig.
She put that bow in the trunk.
Me she put under the bed.

By-and-by—some long time it was—
she took me from under the bed
and did give me a spanking.
She did not have time
to give me a spanking when she
put me under the bed.
She left me there until she did have
time.
After she did it she sent me
to the ranch house to get milk for the
baby.
I walked slow through the oak grove,
looking for caterpillars.
I found nine.

I sit here on the doorstep
printing this on wrapping paper.
The baby is in bed asleep.
The mamma and the rest of the folks
is gone to the ranch house.
She said for me to stay in the doorway
to see that nothing comes
to carry the baby away.
The back part of me feels a little bit
sore,
but I am happy listening
to the twilight music
of God's good world.

The calf is Elizabeth Barrett Browning.
I think she will be a lovely cow.
Her mooings are musical
and there is poetry in her tracks.
She makes such dainty ones.
When they dry up in the lane
I dig them up and save them.
There are lonesome feels in her
mooings
when her mother is away.
I put my arm around her neck.
It is such a comfort to have a friend
near.
when lonesome feels do come.

Jenny Strong visits the mamma.
All her plumpness fills the gray dress
that she wears.
And every time she nods her head
the pink rosebud on her black bonnet
gives itself a nod.
The mamma did spank me because I
showed her my mouse.
She sits by the fire
and rocks and crochets.
She does make lace a quick way.
But I have wonders about her.
She does not like mice.

When I feel sad inside
I talk things over with my tree.
I call him Michael Raphael.
When I go off the barn roof
it is a long jump into his arms.
I might get my leg or my neck broken
and I'd have to keep still for a long
time.
So I always say a little prayer
and do jump in a careful way.
It is such a comfort
to nestle up to Michael Raphael.
He is a grand tree.
He has an understanding soul.

Today the grandpa dug potatoes in
the field.
I followed along after.
I picked them up and piled them in
piles.
Some of them were very plump.
And all the times I was picking up
potatoes
I did have conversations with them.
Too, I did have thinks
of all their growing days there in the
ground,

and all the things they did hear.

Potatoes are very interesting folks.
I think they must see a lot
of what is going on in the earth.
They have so many eyes.
And after, I did count the eyes
that every potato did have,
and their numbers were in blessings.

I have thinks these potatoes growing
here
did have knowings of star-songs.
I have kept watch in the field at night
and I have seen the stars
look kindness down upon them.
And I have walked between the rows
of potatoes
and I have watched the star-gleams
on their leaves.

Dear Love gave me a great big piece
of cheese.
It wasn't a little piece.
There's enough in it for
four breakfasts and six dinners.
Felix Mendelssohn is very happy.
His cheese longings
are like my longings
for Angel Mother and
Angel Father.

Tomorrow I will be taking
the calf, Elizabeth Barrett Browning,
to the girl who has no seeing.
My little friends do like the pats
she gives them
and the words she does say.
She has wants for friends too.

I have need of more color pencils
so I do write the fairies about it.
I put the letter in the moss box
at the end of the old log.
No one knows about the box but one,
he is the man who wears gray neckties
and is kind to mice.

Sometimes he makes a special
fairy wish with me.
I go and tell him
when the fairies leave the pencils.
He is so surprised
and he is happy too.
Then I can make more prints.

Near the trail grow honeysuckles.
I nod to them as I go by.
They talk in shadows
with the little people of the sun.
And this I have learned:
grown-ups do not know the language
of shadows.
Angel Mother and Angel Father did
know

Stockings do have needs of many rubs.
That makes them clean.
While I did do the rubs,
I did sing little songs to the grasses
that grow about our door.

Today I went to Dear Love's house.
She was knitting socks for her
husband.

Opal Whiteley spent nine months piecing together shreds of her childhood diary.

and they taught me.
I wish they were here now.
I do so want them.
I have thinks sometimes
Kind God just opens the gates of
Heaven
and lets them come out to be
Guardian Angels for a while.

I did not have goings to school today,
for this is washday
and the mamma did have needs of me
at home.
There was baby clothes to wash.
The mamma does say that is my work
and I try to do it in the proper way
she does say it ought to be done.
It does take a long time,
and all the time it is taking
I do have longings
to go on exploration trips.

When the clothes of the baby
were most white, I did bring them
again to the wash-bench.
Then there was the chickens to feed,
and the stockings were to rub.

I sat down beside her
right near the blue gingham apron
with cross-stitches on it.
I counted thirty cross-stitches.
Some day I will count them all.

I went to the house of the girl who
has no seeing
but she was not at home.
I did sit on the gatepost to wait waits.
It was a long time.
A man stopped and ask why I wait.
I told him and he looked off to the hills.
Then he did say, "Child, she won't
come back."
I told him I knew she would come
back
because she always does.
I gave him a sorry smile
because he does not know this.
I waited some more waits
and then my mouse made cheese
squeaks.
I will go tomorrow.

Early this morning I went
to the house of

the girl who has no seeing.
Two men were talking by the fence.
One did say, "It is better so."
The other man did say, "A pit tea it was
she couldn't have the sight
to see the bushfire ahead."
Then, "Probably the smell of the smoke
caused her to worry about the house
with the fire coming.
Probably she was trying to find it
when she walked right into it."
And the other man did have asks
if she was con shus after.
He answered "Yes."

I felt a queerness in my throat
and I couldn't see either.
More the men said.
They said all her clothes did have fire,
and her running did make the fire to burn her more.
They found her when she died.

I go now to write a message on a leaf
for the angels to carry her to Heaven
and she can see the blooming flowers.
I will jump into Michael Raphael's arms and talk it over.

One of my tooths is loose and a queer feel.
The man who wears gray neckties
and is kind to mice
says tie a string around it on a doorknob.
I did as he said.
I started to walk off.
Then I came back aways.
I decided to wait a little while.
I walk off again.
Then I took the string off my tooth
and thought I'd wait till after dinner.

On the way home from school
I stop to get watercress for the mamma.
She does have such fondness for it.

Some days are long.
Some days are short.
The days that I have to stay in the house
are the most long days of all.

There are no rows and rows and rows of books in this house
like Angel Mother and Angel Father had.
There is only three books here.
One is a cook-book
and one is a doctor-book
and one is a almanac.
They are all on top of the cupboard
most against the top of the house.

This diary page was written on a paper bag. It says: "Today the folks are gone away from the house we do live in. They are gone a little way away to the ranch house wh"

When the mowers cut down the grain
they also do cut down the cornflowers
that do grow in the fields.
I follow along after and do pick them up.
Of some I make a guirlande
to put around Shakespeare's neck.
Then I do talk to him about the one he is named for.
He is such a beautiful gray horse
and his ways are ways of gentleness.
Too he does have likings
like the likings I have
for the hills that are beyond the fields.

Some day I will write
about the big tree that I love.
Today I watch and did hear its moans
as the saw went through it.
There was a queer feel in my throat
and I couldn't stand up.
When the saw did stop
there was a stillness.
There was a queer sad sound.
The big tree did quiver.
It did sway.
It crashed to the earth.
Oh, Michael Raphael!

Morning work is done.
There is enough barks in the woodbox
for today and tomorrow.
And many kindlings are on the floor.
Now I can make prints.

I am sitting on a log for the last time
in my cathedral.
Tomorrow we will move to a mill town.
Elizabeth Barrett Browning has been sold
with her mother, the gentle jersey.

The man who wears gray neckties
and is kind to mice
is going to take care of all my mouse friends
in his bunkhouse.

Dear Love and her husband
say Felix Mendelssohn can live
under their front step.
They will also take care of my garden.

I have walked past the house
of the girl who has no seeing
and I prayed prayers.
I will leave letters for the fairies
in the moss box.

Dear Love told me a secret.
Only her husband knows.
And now I know.
They are going to have a baby in five months.
The angels let them know ahead.
I have thinks that is a long time to wait waits.
Prayers for babies most always get answered.

Jane Boulton calls herself "a buried poet and novelist." She is now living happily in Palo Alto, California, where she is working on a film script of Opal, *and a novel to be titled,* Journey Within a Journey.

I Remember Grandma

By Loverne Morris

I am 79 years old, have a face like a brown dried apple, and have to rest when my back aches, but I still get a bang out of life. So did Grandma when she was my age. She was 76, and I was almost 10, when I spent a week on the farm with her and Grandpa in 1906. Grandma had 12 children, and outlived six of them. Somehow these deaths didn't destroy Grandma. I think it was partly because she was a strong woman and partly because she got such pleasure out of the creation of a home and a farm on the Kansas frontier.

Grandma said that she and Grandpa built their first cabin on the Illinois prairie, seven miles from the Indiana line, but the country was low, and they had ague (malaria) and other sicknesses, so they decided to go to Kansas to get healthy land.

When I spent that week at Grandma's house when I was 10, she showed me the date carved in the stone sill of the east window upstairs. It said 1875. That was the year that she and Grandpa had built the house from stone that they had quarried themselves from the north hill of the farm. They hired a mason only to smooth the facing stones for doors and windows. Under the lee of the big stone house was the springhouse, where water piped from a nearby spring flowed over a stone ledge. Here, large pans of milk were set for the cream to rise to the top. Not far away was the cyclone cellar, a cave where we could take refuge in big storms.

All were enchanting places to me. I loved to race all over the farmhouse, up to the attic (where I found Grandma's spinning wheel and her 1860s black silk dress with its hooped skirt and black jet buttons) through the long hall past the hired man's room and the boys' room and the girls' room and the guest room, and down the crooked stairs. In the parlor I loved to finger the organ and look at the painted vase of pampas plumes on top, I remember a dark-red plush settee and matching chairs, two Boston rockers, a base burner with a shield to protect the flowered carpet, family pictures in oval walnut frames, a big Bible and picture album on a little table. Hanging from the ceiling was a wonderful lamp with a painted glass shade and clinking crystal pendants. Above the bookcase was a hair wreath made of many colors of human hair.

Across the stairwell from the living room downstairs was my grandparents' bedroom with its wide stone fireplace. Grandma would rock in front of the fire there while she combed and braided my hair. Then we would go through the big

The stone house near Emporia, Kansas, built by Theodore and Edna Castle Little, grandparents of the author, is a landmark.

room where Thanksgiving dinners were spread, through the everyday dining room and out to the well, where Grandma would draw up the bucket and water the lilies of the valley and the pansies around the well curb.

When I wanted a juicy winesap apple, I could go down to the cool apple cellar where they were stored. Once during that memorable week I had a scare there. As I started back up the stairs, I saw a five-foot black snake stretched on a beam above my head. "Grandma!" I yelled, and she came and assured me that the black snakes did not bite, and I could come up. I bent my head and dashed up and outdoors while Grandma dispatched the critter.

In the kitchen of the stone house, there was a big black Majestic range burning wood or coal, but Grandma told me she had cooked over the fireplace when she first came to Kansas in 1859. She showed me the candlesticks she had used before she had lamps, and showed me her first dash churn. By 1906, when I was there, she used a barrel churn for her butter, and I turned it until my arm grew tired. I liked to watch Grandma as she salted and paddled the pale yellow butter until it was firm, then packed it in stoneware crocks to put in the springhouse.

Saturday was bath day. Grandma and I carried warm water to the guest room, and she poured it into a huge flowered bowl set on a mat on the floor beside the commode. She saw to it that I scrubbed well with soap, then she dried my back with a towel softer than the huck and grainsack towels in the kitchen.

Afternoons, I swung in a barrel-stave hammock that hung between a sycamore and an elm tree in the front yard. Or Grandma and I would go the the orchard to pick fruit, and she would tell me how she had planted the apple and cherry and apricot and peach trees there. She said it was a big satisfaction to watch trees grow, and to harvest fruit and to put up many hundreds of jars of jams and preserves. In the early days, she recalled, she'd had to depend on wild berries, wild plums and wild grapes, and in 1860 there had been a terrible drought—no crops, wild fruit, or game at all. Some settlers nearly starved. That was when she and Grandpa packed the covered wagon and went to her parents in Indiana for the winter.

When they returned the next spring, they brought back an organ which Grandma said was a big help when she opened a Sunday school and a subscription day-school in her cabin. Parents paid a dollar for three months of schooling for each child. (Money was worth a lot then. For instance, my granparents paid just a dollar an acre for their first 80 acres of Kansas land.) Grandma was a fine speller, and she said that every child in her school learned to spell. She tried to get me to spell syllable-style, but my tongue got twisted.

This is Grandma, Edna Castle Little, born in Indiana in 1830. Her granddaughter calls her "the most courageous and remarkable woman I have ever known; a strong pioneer woman who achieved equality in marriage."

Grandma had a good relationship with the Indians in the area. Some of them would peek in the window at Grandma's school. And many times I heard the story of the time the Indians "borrowed" my mother when she was a baby, nine months old, in the spring of 1866. An old Indian couple had been coming to the house often to trade berries or nuts for *copsie* (coffee) or salt pork, and Grandma had found the old couple trustworthy. So, when the woman wanted to show the white-skinned baby to the band of Kaws camped at the creek, Grandma allowed it. But she sent her older children along to watch over the baby. They found the Indians sitting around a campfire where a pot of stew was bubbling. Hidden behind trees, they watched as each Indian took the baby, clucked and grinned and passed her on around the circle. At first the baby liked it, but when she got wet, she cried, and then the Indians let the older kids take the baby home. Grandma was pretty relieved to get her back.

Grandma did not say much about the really bad times, but my aunties had told me about the time when war raiders came into Kansas, and about the big prairie fire of 1862, and the 1874 grasshopper plague that stripped off every green leaf, and the cyclone that just missed the cabin, and about the smallpox and diptheria epidemics. Grandma told my only the good things: what it was like selling butter and eggs in town and selling cheese to the men who were making the railroad; working to get money to buy more land, and to educate the children, and provide good books and magazines for the family.

Grandpa was more easygoing than Grandma. He was big and slow. He worked hard at a steady pace but with less display of energy than Grandma, who was small, blond, and quick. He said the blessing at meal, led family worship at night, and played hymns on his violin. He played jigs, too, and liked to tell quaint little jokes and riddles. While he was doing that, Grandma would be mending or knitting mittens or socks. On Sunday, the team of strong gray horses took us in the spring wagon up the stony road to Bethel Church.

Friends of my grandparents', plain country men and women, sang in the choir, and they did not always sing on key. While the preacher was giving his long, tiresome sermon, I would look out the windows and listen to the bees in the churchyard clover and the calling of the doves.

A few times in my youth I encountered death in the family. There was sorrow for dear ones lost to us, but I never sensed fear of death in Grandma's house.

There were a dozen family graves in the nearby cemetery and on Decoration Day the family went and cleared the wild grass from the graves and put flowers on them. When one of my aunties died, I saw the Bethel choir women stand by the casket in Grandma'a parlor and sing "Nearer My God to Thee," with tears streaming down their faces. The preacher said, "The Lord giveth and the Lord taketh away."

I remember a Thanksgiving Day at the farm when about three dozen of the family and the preacher and his wife were there. The daughters and daughters-in-law baked pies and cakes and hams that they brought for the feast. When we arrived that morning, the turkey, full of Grandma's famous stuffing, would be roasting and giving off tantalizing odors.

At one o'clock the goodies were on the tables, Grandpa said the blessing, and we got down to the business of eating. The grown-ups sat at the long trestle table that was set up in the big room, and we children had a table in the dining room, with the double doors open between. I ate and ate until I literally felt I would burst. After dinner, the boy cousins would wad pieces of Grandma's fresh-baked bread and throw them at us. We girls kicked the boys under the table. Then the dishes were pushed aside, and we all went to the old barn.

In earlier years Grandpa and Grandma had many cows, horses, and hogs. Grandma never milked or cared for stock or did fieldwork except in emergencies, but she knew how to do almost anything. One time I tried to milk Rosy the cow but only got a teacup of milk, and she jerked her head and switched her tail to say I was a nuisance.

Grandma still had a dozen laying hens and a couple of biddies with chicks. When I picked up a chick, I would get pecked and scolded by the mama. But Grandma let me feed and water the chickens and gather the eggs. I also helped Grandma pull weeds in the flower beds and garden. (I remember that I was a bit startled when she made her long full dark skirt into a tent and irrigated the flowers, saving a trip to the outhouse.)

Everyone worked at work time, Grandma had taught all her children to work, and the grandchildren also were expected to help with chores. But when work was over, there was apt to be singing around the organ. Grandmother's fingers were as creaky as mine are now, but she could still play the organ and sing. She taught me Stephen Foster songs like "Oh! Susanna," "Old Black Joe," and "Home Sweet Home."

When the town's important citizens came to visit her, they all dined on Grandma's bone china with sterling silver knives and forks and coin-silver spoons. I remember Grandma wore her heavy black taffeta dress with the basque waist, the leg-of-mutton sleeves, and the lace at the throat. Everything was served in proper style, and Grandma would converse on many subjects of the day.

Grandma looked so fine. She not only took care of herself, but she also made me wear my sunbonnet when I went outdoors. (A tan was not admired in those days.) She also saw to it that I ate vegetables and fruit to balance the salt pork and milk gravy we had at least once a day.

There were always lots of interesting things around the old stone house. Though she no longer used them,

The author, Loverne Morris, as she looked in 1975. Now 85-years-old, she says "my energy is diminished, but I still write some, sell local history stories, and belong to a couple of historical societies. That is enough about me."

Grandma still had the three-legged soap kettle and the three-legged dutch oven with the curved lid, both of which she had brought to Kansas in the covered wagon. There were also the maul and broadax and other tools Grandpa had used to build the first cabin and break the sod. In the cupboard in Grandma's bedroom I found a doctor book, which I used to read in secret. I skipped the chapters on remedies for whooping cough, measles, and scarlet fever because the chapter on marriage and childbirth was much more exciting. When I heard Grandma coming, I hastily put it back; I did not want to get spanked.

After our 1906 Thanksgiving, Grandpa and Grandma sold their farm and moved to town. Grandpa did not know what to do in town. He died soon after they moved, but Grandma lived more than two years longer. She broke her hip some months before her death, and a young woman was hired to take care of her. That was not easy, for Grandma would not mind anyone. People would quit sooner than put up with Grandma's spirited ways.

I remember the last day I ever spent with her. When I arrived, Grandma was dozing in her bed by the south window in the big living room. Her yellowish-white hair was braided and her eyes and her face came alive. She told me to take a stick of horehound candy from the stand by her bed. As I chewed the bittersweet stick, she suddenly pulled herself up by a bedpost, and said, "Fetch me the tall stool by the kitchen sink." Bewildered, I brought it. Then she ordered, "Get me those two canes behind that door." I obeyed, but said in fright, "You mustn't get out of bed!"

"Nonsense, I've done it before." Grasping me, she pulled herself out of bed onto the stool, chest down, and had me give her the canes. Ignoring my protest, she moved herself slowly to the kitchen and said, "Stir up the range fire and put in some coal. I'm going to make an apple pie." She had me bring the apples, flour, salt, lard, rolling pin, and pie tins. Then she let me peel and slice the apples while she made the piecrust. She spilled the water a bit because her hands shook as mine do now. But she made a perfect pie and she told me, "A fruit pie needs a hot fire. Spit on the stove lid to see if it sizzles." I did as she said and watched the water dance on the range top. "Pop the pie into the oven and get me back to bed," she barked, "and don't you dare say a word of this to anyone." Guiltily, I obeyed. When I got her into bed, her eyes fluttered shut and she was breathing hard. I was scared. But her eyes opened and she said shortly, "Take the pie out in forty minutes and cut it in quarters. We'll each have a piece."

When the pie was baked and flaky-crisp and fragrant, I cut it and Grandma had me bring clotted cream from the icebox. We put a spoonful of cream on top and we each ate a fourth of that pie and then sighed with contentment. I washed up and put the kitchen in order and was just leaving when the nursemaid came in. Grandma winked at me and put a finger on her lips.

I did not sleep much that night. I woke up after dreaming that all the family was called to Grandma's death-bed. I ached to unburden my guilty feelings at the breakfast table, but I kept Grandma's secret until this day. She lived three or four months after that before she went to sleep for good. And as far as I know, the pie-making didn't hurt her a bit.

Loverne Morris was 85 in 1982, and she still writes and sells her stories. Her writing has ranged from children's bedtime stories (1920s), radio serials (1930s), news features (1940s), and most recently books on local California history, crafts, and skills. She has eight grandchildren, six great-grandchildren, and lives in Rainbow Hill Valley, near Fallbrook, California.

DOROTHY BROWN

A DOCTOR FOR THE PEOPLE

By Elizabeth Levy & Mara Miller

Dr. Dorothy Brown is 59 years old, black, and a woman—the first black woman to practice general surgery in the South. She is also the first black woman ever to win an election and sit in the Tennessee State Legislature.

She is a broad-boned and wide-shouldered smiling figure in a white doctor's coat. That coat must be famous among Nashville cleaners because throughout our interview Dr. Brown jots down names, numbers, and notes to herself on the hem of her coat.

Dr. Brown's story, however, is not on the hem of her lab coat. "When I was a youngster, I was a complete extrovert, growing up

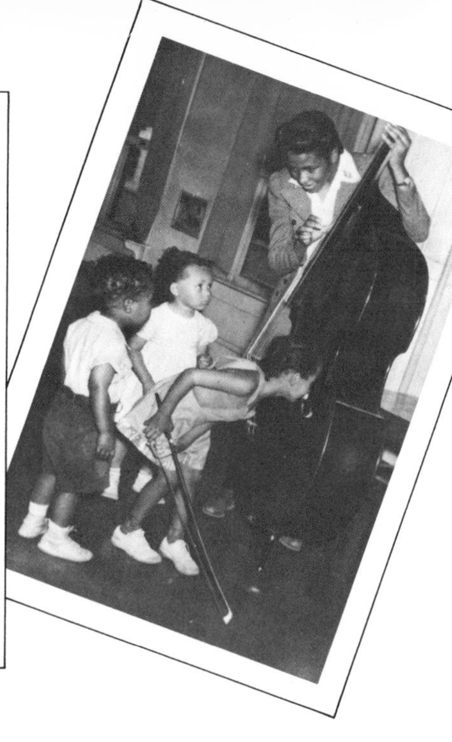

At 14, I worked as a servant in Lake George, New York (*left*); at 16, I graduated from Troy High School (*center*); at Bennett College, I was a member of the string ensemble (*right*).

in a sea of white people. I was in an orphanage in Troy, New York, with about 350 kids, and only six of us were blacks. If you had enough colds during the school year, then when school closed you were selected to have your tonsils and adenoids out. When I was five, they sent me to the hospital for that and I caused quite a stir. I insisted that I wanted to make the rounds with the nurses, and I wanted to use the doctor's stethoscope and carry my chart into the operating room.

"You see, I was completely oblivious to the business of race. I was enthusiastic and enthralled by the sights and smells of medicine. I wanted to be a doctor from then on. I didn't even think in terms of being a nurse. I wanted to be the chief head-knocker.

"Nobody laughed at me. At that orphanage we were encouraged constantly to assess what we wanted to become. So when I was five and said I wanted to become a doctor, there was no one to say, 'Why, that's insane! Why don't you be more practical?'

"There was a policy at the orphanage that when black kids reached about fourteen or fifteen, they'd be farmed out to work in the wealthy homes in the neighborhood to learn how to be cooks, maids, and butlers.

"During the summers and after school, I was working as a maid. All the people I worked for knew I was trying to save money for college, so when I said to them, 'Will you let me try to do a whole day's work in just half a day, but pay me for the whole day?' they agreed. The work was very heavy physically and quite demanding.

"One day this lady I worked for told me that the Methodist Women of Troy Conference was looking for a black girl to send to Bennett College in Greensboro, North Carolina, all expenses paid. The college was named for a local Troy minister, and in all the years, the Methodist Women had never had a black—well, we were 'Negroes' at that time—they had never had a Negro girl attend this college. So I met with them in the middle of August, and that's how I got to college."

After college, Dr. Brown trained at the Meharry Medical College in Nashville. Then she came back north to intern at Harlem Hospital in New York.

"At the end of my internship I sought a residency in general surgery at Harlem Hospital. Of course, that was insane. They were just not going to have a woman. So I turned to Meharry, where I had done my medical training. Matthew Walker, who was chief of surgery, was a little amused, but he asked his staff anyway, and of course they said that a woman could not withstand the

One of my classes at Meharry Medical College in 1958.

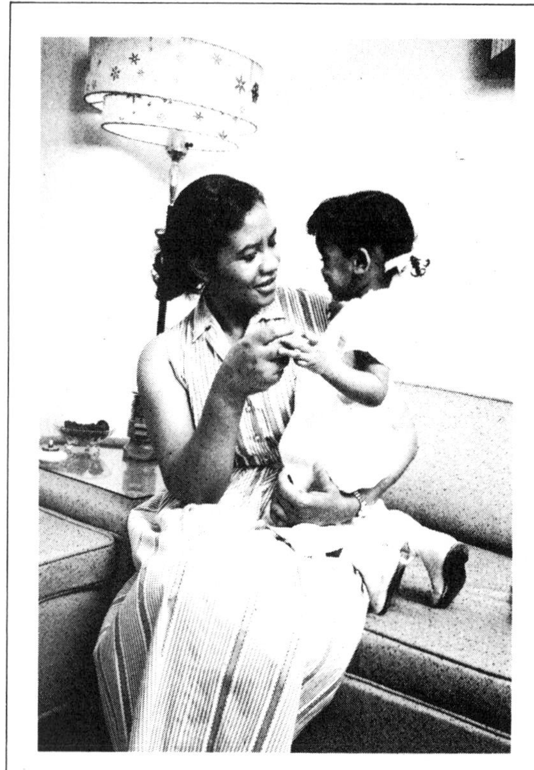

My daughter and myself at home in 1958.

physical rigors of five years of training in general surgery.

"But I was pretty insistent, and so Dr. Walker decided to try me, and there were no rigors whatsoever. Of course, there were not going to be any as far as I was concerned, because I was bound, bent, and determined that if necessary I would overcompensate to see to it that I made it.

"I'll never forget one Saturday night when I was chief resident in general surgery and I had just finished a series of emergency cases with an assistant. We were on our way over to the cafeteria and then were going to go get some sleep.

"All of a sudden, the Emergency Room had another case and this fellow who was going to assist me turned and said, 'Dee, I hate to admit this to you, but I just can't go any further.'

"I was tired too, but I said, 'That's okay, just go on ahead.' It was just fortunate that I was the mule who could carry on. There was no crying or getting emotionally disturbed, because I knew the job I had to do, and I went forward to do it.

"Since that episode my word to women students is that when you pass through the doors at seven or eight in the morning, you are not a woman, you're a doctor.

"I've never married and I won't deny that probably the most outstanding thing about my desire to be married was that I wanted children. I was lucky in that I had the opportunity to adopt my daughter at birth. Even now I wouldn't want to be married because the only thing I'd be marrying for now would be companionship. And I don't need it. I would feel sorry for a man who would be married to me, because it would have been impossible for a man to have stopped me.

"When I became chief of surgery here at Riverside Hospital in Nashville, I recall one time a fellow said to me that he didn't like me because I was too aggressive. So I said to him, 'You have to remember that you guys were the ones who made me aggressive.'

"I had one man, an elderly man who had a preoperative diagnosis of a ruptured appendix. I was chief resident at the time, which means that I had nine to eleven fellows working under me, but, of course, as chief resident I was charged with doing the surgery on the poor risk cases. So I went around to the ward to take a look at this poor risk old gent before I operated on him and he looked up at me and said, '*You're* not going to operate on me?'

"I said, 'Oh, yes, I am, sir.'

"He said, 'You'd better get one of these fellows to

At my desk in the Lower House of the Tennessee Legislature in 1966.

operate on me because you ain't nothing but a little old girl, and you don't know what you're doing.'

"I said, 'Okay.' I let the fellows go on and work him up, and I just waited until he got to the operating room, then I operated on him. . . . I told him afterward.

"I recall when I began private practice, one of the doctors said, 'Dee, I wouldn't start to practice medicine in Nashville. People are not accustomed to a woman surgeon; you'll starve to death.' But it hasn't happened. My first year of practice, I had about forty percent male and sixty percent female patients. Right now I have as many male patients as I have females. And though most of them are black, I have a fair share of whites, too, even though my office is in the black community.

"Of course, I've had to beat the bushes looking for my own surgical cases. If I sat back and waited for referrals, I probably *would* starve. So I do a lot of general medicine practice too. I just see anybody who wants to see a doctor. If it's something I can handle, then I go ahead and do it; if it's something I don't want to handle, like asthma and all that stuff, then I refer them. But what I want to do is surgery.

"One of the reasons I went into a specialty instead of going into the immensity of general practice was that I was just afraid I didn't know enough medicine to save enough people.

"There's no use my telling a lie. When I lose a patient, I spend the rest of that night going through that patient's records to see if I have made a mistake, to see if there wasn't something else that I could have done that would have spelled the difference between life and death. These things weigh upon me and I think this is one of the reasons that I work so hard."

Because she was so well known in the community, Dr. Brown was asked to run for the seat in Nashville's predominantly black state lower house district. Although some of the local Democratic political bosses were against her, she won both the primary and the general election with ease and became the first black woman in the Tennessee Legislature.

She stayed relatively quiet in government for a year, learning the ropes. But then, just at the end of the first session, in 1967, she dropped a bombshell: she introduced a bill to reform the state's antiquated abortion laws. Remember that this was more than 10 years ago and Tennessee law forbade all abortions, except if the life of the mother was in danger. Far from granting abortion on demand, Dr. Brown's bill would have allowed abortions in cases of rape and incest. Yet she knew that even this small change in the law would meet great resistance.

"I knew it was going to be a hell of a thing, because after all, Tennessee is one of the Bible states," said Dr. Brown. "Most white women had no problem, but the poor whites and the black women had problems getting abortions, because they didn't have the money. And the thing that really stirred me was when I figured out how much an abortionist in the black market made. The lowest figure was $350, and any abortionist worth his salt could be doing at least six a day. I said, 'This is ridiculous. This is stupid. Why don't I do something about it?'

"I feel there are certain things, certain issues, that you have to address yourself to in this life, and if you're rational about it, then you don't turn back."

The bill actually almost got passed, losing by only two votes. But for Dr. Brown, it was the end of her legislative career. "I've paid the price over and over again. I don't think I'll ever be able to gain political office, unless an ultimate disposition of the whole question of abortion is made, because every time I pop up, the first thing they think about is the abortion issue."

Since 1968, Dr. Brown has run three times for her old seat and lost.

"No, I haven't accepted defeat, not in my entire life. The only defeat I understand is physical defeat. To me it's a grievous sin for people to waste the days of their lives, and not to do something that makes the world a little better, or at least notifies the world that you've been around."

Elizabeth Levy has written over twenty books for children and teenagers, including the popular "Something Queer" mystery series.

Mara Miller's recent book is Where to Go for What: How to Research, Organize and Present Your Ideas.

BY LETTY COTTIN POGREBIN

"Whenever I play baseball with my brother and I get a hit, he says it was luck. But if I strike out it's because of my sex. Click!"
–Moira Brennan, Providence, R.I.

All over the country, girls like Moira Brennan are hearing the *click* that tells them something unfair is going on. If a girl wants to play sports, she has a problem even before she tries out for a team. Boys have to worry about being good enough to play. But girls have to worry about being *allowed to prove* that they're good enough to play.

Thousands of girls are beginning to fight back. They are challenging old-fashioned ideas—like the belief that girls are too fragile, or the myth that girls are never as good as boys in athletics. Many of these young women have written to *Ms.* to share their anger and their plans for action.

Kelly Kirk of Winona, Minnesota, writes: "In junior high there are no sports (basketball, volleyball, softball, track) for girls. It's time for those of us who enjoy sports to start hollering."

Deirdre Garvey, 14, of Princeton, New Jersey, tells of an incident in coed track and field: "My gym teacher (male) told us that the boys would put an 8-pound shot, and the girls would put a 6-pound shot. I went over to one of the boys and asked him to give me the 8-pound shot. I walked over to the circle, spun around, and put the 8-pound shot. I made 21 feet. The gym teacher refused to comment. Later, in class, some of the boys started to ask me, 'Do you want to be a man when you grow up?' I told them I was a woman and proud of it."

Pat Viera of Pasadena, California, 18, writes: "I would like someday to coach a National Basketball Association team, but I can't. I'd love to go to some big college on an athletic scholarship and eventually play on a professional team, but I can't. I'm not mentally or physically handicapped, but I'm a girl. . . ."

While these girls and young women are fighting their private battles, one battle has been fought in public and the whole country has watched its outcome.

The Little League—which puts more than 2 million 8- to 12-year-old *boys* on baseball fields in 31 countries—has finally agreed to accept girls.

It all began in New Jersey in 1972, when a young ballplayer named Maria Pepe was accepted by the Hoboken Little League team. Maria's teammates had no objections to her, but the men in charge at the national headquarters of Little League refused to let the Hoboken team stay in the league if they kept a girl in their ranks.

The case eventually went to court and the judges decided that it was against the law for Little League to stop any child from joining a team just because she happens to be a girl. This court decision was greeted with mixed notices. In New York, the American Civil Liberties Union went to bat for seven girls, while families in other states turned to the National Organization for Women or to private lawyers to help their daughters break the sex barrier. Teams were disbanded, new teams took their place. Some Little Leagues voluntarily "desexegrated" while others insisted on keeping girls behind the fences.

In New Jersey, throughout last spring, 2,000 teams refused to play rather than accept girls. There were angry demonstrations and arguments among parents. Some communities were fiercely split down the middle and through it all, individual girls, like those quoted below, experienced the joys and embarrassment of being "female firsts" in a formerly male preserve.

Then, last June, officials of Little League Baseball, Inc., announced that they would "defer to the changing social climate" and let girls play on their teams.

Meanwhile, the Babe Ruth Baseball League (whose program serves 300,000 boys from 13 to 18 years old) still refuses to change their "boys only" rule, and countless local city and town teams continue to bar girls from the fields.

No one can guess how long it will be before "batter up" means *her* as well as *him*. But until then, there will be gutsy girls and young women taking to the playing fields, at the same time that they work to change attitudes and laws.

Here are some of the trailblazers—the young players who believe that *baseball* diamonds are a girl's best friend. When the first female hero is nominated for the Baseball Hall of Fame, she may well be one of these spirited girls who have fought their way out of the bleachers and into the action.

Dawna Ethier, 13. Nashua, New Hampshire. Last year I got an application to play for the Little League Yankees, but my parents wouldn't sign it. They thought the game was too rough. Then I started playing hockey.

Finally my mom said it was okay for me to try out if I could talk my dad into it, and I did. I made it through tryouts against a lot of boys. I played the whole season—I guess about 30 games altogether—and my batting average was .450.

Since I was the only girl in the whole league, some of the pitchers would hit me to make me cry. But I just took my base, no matter how much it hurt.

I think that if a girl can beat boys, she should be allowed to try. Maybe you have to go through a hassle, but it's worth it. I don't think any girl should have to pretend to be a boy, though. I got my ears pierced because I want to look like a girl no matter what I do on the field.

This year I played all-girl basketball and hockey, and I'm also helping mentally retarded kids. When I grow up I want to be a physical education teacher and help girls go out for any sport they like. Any sport at all.

Ellen Vetromile, 12. Ho-ho-kus, New Jersey. I pitch or I play shortstop for the Eagles, which is a Youth Activities Council team in our town. The boys don't tease me at all, but the fathers of the boys on the opposite team yell at me from the bleachers. They'll say, "Go on home and help your mother do the dishes," and stuff like that. They're razzing me because I'm better than their sons, and they can't stand it.

My parents are real proud of me. My mother comes to most of me a lot, so I had to wear dresses to prove to them I was a girl. People are always calling me a tomboy. I think it would be pretty wild if women could just do what we want. I play tennis, tackle football, and I was on a championship hockey team. I don't think women are too feminine to do anything!

Maureen Gorman, 11. Trenton, New Jersey. I was looking in the papers day in and day out, thinking maybe, maybe, maybe they'll really let girls play Little League. two games. But the other parents didn't want a girl on the team with their sons. They fired the manager and canceled the record of the games we won when I was on the team.

I'm not really angry. I don't care any more. Maybe they said nasty things behind my back, but I never heard them. I just felt stupid seeing my picture on everything, and I got tired of the publicity. If I had a little girl who wanted to play ball, maybe I'd go to court for her. Probably I would.

my games. My brother plays catcher or second base. He's about 15, and he says I'm as good as he was at 12.

Jennifer Baad, 12. Battle Creek, Michigan. In 1972, my mother, my brother, and I drove over to tryouts for the Empire Little League. I had a shag haircut, and I said my name was Jay. I made the team real easy.

All summer long they thought I was a boy. Once I went to my brother's tennis tournament, and one boy from my team saw me in a halter top, but he never told.

Finally, the coach found out I was a girl when he read a story in the Detroit Free Press. By then I had played the whole season.

Some of my girlfriends teased When they made the court decision, I joined the Hamilton Jewelers team. I play second base, and my brother Jimmy catches for another team in the same league. Sometimes we play against each other, but that's okay.

My parents like me to play ball. They were real glad to see me up and around again. Last August I was in the hospital with meningitis, which is almost as bad as polio.

I'd like to go out for the Babe Ruth League, but I don't think they'll take girls by the time I'm 13.

Sharon Poole, 15. Haverhill, Massachusetts. Back in 1971 when I was 12, the coach of the Haverhill Little League Indians asked me to try out. I played center field in

A couple of girls tried to go to Indians tryouts the year after me, but there was a big sign up that said NO GIRLS ALLOWED. Last year, no girls even tried.

Sheila O'Donnell, 14. Schenectady, New York. Last year they wouldn't let me play on the Babe Ruth League team, so my mom and I decided to try for bigger and better things.

Mom is really gung ho. She's been on two radio shows talking about girls' sports. We started a summer soccer league for girls and a basketball clinic. Then we made up a group called EGOS, which stands for Encourage Girls' Organized Sports. EGOS is a pressure group, and we sure put pressure on the Guilderland School

System, where I live.

Last year the budget for girls' sports was $1,000. We got them up to $11,000 for 1974-75. We also got them to hire a director of women's intramurals and interscholastic activities and to expand the program in field hockey, track, and softball.

We don't want to get into boys' sports. We just want strong equitable treatment and facilities for girls. All my girlfriends are athletic, too, and we're sick and tired of seeing boys do what we can't.

Carolyn King, 12. Ypsilanti, Michigan. When the order came from national Little League headquarters that the Orioles had to drop me, my coaches, Mr. Harry Spires and Mr. Wayne Warren, really stuck by me. So did the city council of Ypsilanti and the newspapers.

But the team lost its charter, so now we're not in Little League any more. We're a youth league financed by the city, and we're open to all boys and girls. I'm sure glad that women are finally getting their rights.

Baseball is just one of my interests. I have a 94 average, and I also play the violin.

Yvonne Burch, 14. Concord, North Carolina. There's nothing to do around here in the summertime so last year I went down to the baseball field and asked if I could just practice with the team. They let me play second base and sometimes catch.

Then the coach decided to take me on. The boys knew my playing style because I'd played with them in school for years. I did pretty good on the team. The only razzing I got was from the stands. If I struck out, someone would yell "Hey, girl, y'all not be playin' anyway."

One day some man from Trenton threatened to cancel the club's Babe Ruth League charter, so I had to leave the team. Now we're waiting for advice from a lawyer.

There's an all-girls' softball league around here, but it's stupid. They make you use an underhand pitch, and they don't let you steal or slide. They take all the fun out of the game just because they think it's too rough for girls.

Juliet Luther, 8. Randolph, New Jersey. It was my own idea to go out for the Hawks.

I'm the only girl on the team. Nobody pays any attention to it. I get to play a lot of ball because we have three practice sessions and on Saturday we play a game. I'm learning how to bunt.

Felicia Lee, 12. Teaneck, New Jersey. I was listening to the radio every day waiting for the court decision. When I heard that girls could play, I tried out. I've wanted to play Little League ball since I was seven.

Girls' softball isn't nearly as much fun. In Little League you play with a hardball; you get to play more games; and they give you uniforms and trophies.

After I made the team, I read in the New York Times that my manager said he didn't want me on the team. I just laughed.

In my second game, I hit a 200-foot home run. Now my batting average is about .300.

I'm the only girl on my team, but the boys treat me just like one of them. Pitchers on opponents' teams sometimes hit me on a pitch. Them hardballs don't tickle. I don't think they're doing it on purpose, but I got ways of finding that out. If they are doing it, I can bat that hardball right back into their faces if I have to.

Later, I want to be a stewardess. But now I want to play baseball and run track in the Olympics.

Letty Cottin Pogrebin, a Ms. editor, is also the author of Growing Up Free: Raising Your Child in the 80s.

Fun, Facts, and Feelings

Part 3

IRA SLEEPS OVER

BY BERNARD WABER

I was invited to sleep at Reggie's house.
Was I happy!
I had never slept at a friend's house before. But I had a problem.
It began when my sister said:
"Are you taking your teddy bear along?"
"Taking my teddy bear along!" I said.
"To my friend's house? Are you kidding?
That's the silliest thing I ever heard!
Of course, I'm not taking my teddy bear."
And then she said:
"But you never slept without your teddy bear before.
How will you feel sleeping without your teddy bear for the very first time?
Hmmmmmmm?"
"I'll feel fine. Just don't worry about it," I said.
But now she had me thinking about it.
I began to wonder:

Suppose I just hate sleeping without my teddy bear.
Should I take him?
"Take him," said my mother.
"Take him," said my father.
"But Reggie will laugh," I said. "He'll say I'm a baby."
"He won't laugh," said my mother.
"He won't laugh," said my father.
"He'll laugh," said my sister.
I decided not to take my teddy bear.
That afternoon, I played with Reggie.
Reggie had plans, big plans.
"Tonight," he said, "when you come to my house, we are going to have fun, fun, fun."
"Great!" I said. "I can hardly wait."
"By the way," I asked, "what do you think of teddy bears?"
But Reggie just went on talking and planning as if he had never heard of teddy bears.
"And do you know what we can do when the lights are out and the house is really dark?"
"What?" I asked.
"We can tell ghost stories," said Reggie, "scary, creepy, spooky ghost stories."
I began to think about my teddy bear.
"Does your house get very dark?" I asked.

"Uh-huh," said Reggie.
"By the way," I said again, "what do you think of teddy bears?"
Suddenly, Reggie was in a big hurry to go someplace.
"See you tonight," he said.
I decided to take my teddy bear.
"Good," said my mother.
"Good," said my father. But my sister said:
"What if Reggie wants to know your teddy bear's name.
And did you think about how he will laugh and say Tah Tah is a silly, baby name, even for a teddy bear?"
I decided not to take my teddy bear.
At last it was time to go to Reggie's house.
I went next door where Reggie lived.
That night, Reggie showed me his junk. He showed me his flashlight, his collection of bottle caps, jumbo goggles, a false nose and mustache, and a bunch of old rubber stamps.
We decided to play "office"
with the rubber stamps.
After that we had a wrestling match.
And after that we had a pillow fight. And after that Reggie's father said:
"Bedtime!"
We got into bed.
Reggie began to tell a ghost story:

"Once there was this ghost and he lived in a haunted house . . .
This house was empty except for this ghost because nobody wanted to go near this house, they were so afraid of this ghost.
And every night this ghost would go around looking for
people to scare. And he was very scary
to look at. Oh,
was he scary. . . ."
Reggie stopped.
"Are you scared?" he asked.
"Uh-huh," I said. "Are you?"
"Just a minute," said Reggie, "I have to get something."
Reggie pulled something out of a drawer.
The room was dark,
but I could see it had fuzzy arms and legs
and was about the size of a teddy bear.
I looked again. It was a teddy bear.
Reggie got back into bed.
"Is that your teddy bear?" I asked.
"You mean this teddy bear?"
"The one you're holding," I said.
"Uh-huh," Reggie answered.
"Do you sleep with him all of the time?"

"Uh-huh."
"Does your teddy bear have a name?" I said.
"Uh-huh," Reggie answered.
"What is it?"
"You won't laugh?" said Reggie.
"No, I won't laugh," I said.
"It's Foo Foo."
"Did you say 'Foo Foo'?"
"Uh-huh," said Reggie.
"Just a minute," I said, "I have to get something."
The next minute, I was ringing my own doorbell.
"Ira!" everyone said. "What are you doing here?"
"I changed my mind," I said. "I decided to take Tah Tah after all."
I came back to Reggie's room. I looked at Reggie. He was fast asleep.
Just like that, he had fallen asleep.
"Reggie! Wake up!" I said. "You have to finish telling the ghost story."
But Reggie just held his teddy bear closer and went right on sleeping.
And after that—
Well, there wasn't anything to do after that.
"Good night," I whispered to Tah Tah.
And I fell asleep, too.

Bernard Waber is the author of several children's books including Lyle, Lyle Crocodile; Dear Hildegarde; *and* Bernard. Bernard *is about a dog who is the center of a custody battle. Waber is also on the staff of* Time, *where he art-directs magazine layout.*

STORIES FOR FREE CHILDREN

LIKE IT IS:
Facts and Feelings About Handicaps From Kids Who Know

By Barbara Adams
Photographs by James Stanfield

I'm Jed.

I've got Legg-Perthes Disease. I got it two years ago, when I was six. It's a disease that affects the top of the thigh bone (femur) and the hip joint. The braces take pressure off the bones so they can heal properly. In a few years I'll be able to walk normally again.

I'm glad about that. Wearing braces can be a drag, especially when they keep you from doing something fun. Or when people look at you funny or are afraid of you. I don't like that, but I understand why it happens. When I first saw my friend Jon, I never thought *I* would be friends with him. And Marielle, who's got cerebral palsy—she walks and talks like a broken puppet.

Those kids were scary to me at first. I guess I thought that because they looked different on the outside, they might be strange on the inside. But once I got to know them, all that changed.

The word *handicap* * means something that hinders you, something that gets in your way sometimes. An *orthopedic handicap* means that some part of your body can't move in the usual way.

Often, the person is born with the problem. But it can also occur because of an accident or an illness. One thing for sure, neither the orthopedic problem nor the illness that caused it is *catching.*

When I first met Jon, I had the weird feeling that if I hung around with him, maybe my legs would get worse and I'd become like he is. I already had my braces, and I knew I wasn't going to have to wear them all my life. I also knew I couldn't catch what Jon had from being with him. So why did I feel like that?

*Many prefer the term "disabled." See the "Resolution on Disabled Women," passed at the National Women's Conference in November, 1977, at Houston, Texas. (Reported in *Ms.*, March, 1978.)

My dad explained that everybody has a primitive part of his or her brain that sometimes has illogical thoughts that aren't true in reality. These thoughts can give a person some strange feelings. My dad said that whenever I have uncomfortable feelings that don't make sense, I should talk them over with him. And he suggested that I try to get to know Jon.

Well, I became friends with Jon, and he's a neat guy. I don't have any of the feelings I started out with now that I know him.

Jon had an illness called *peroneal muscular atrophy,* which injured the nerves that carry the signals from his brain to his legs. When nerves are damaged, the signals are not passed along to the muscles, so the muscles don't move. They are *paralyzed.* A paralyzed muscle doesn't grow or develop. That's why Jon's legs are thin and small.

Jon used to go to a school for handicapped kids only. One day he

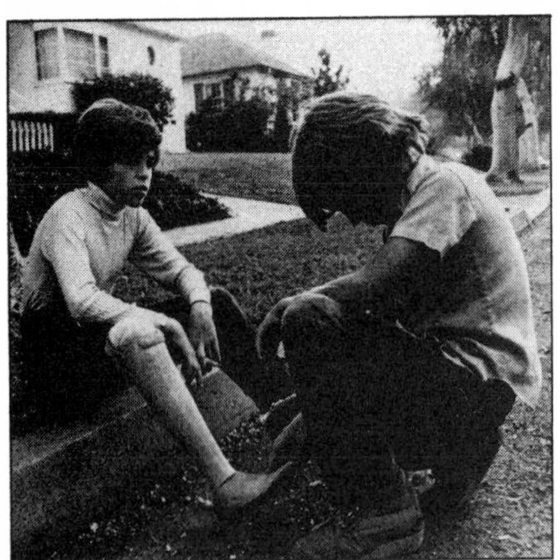

Andre shows how his prosthesis works.

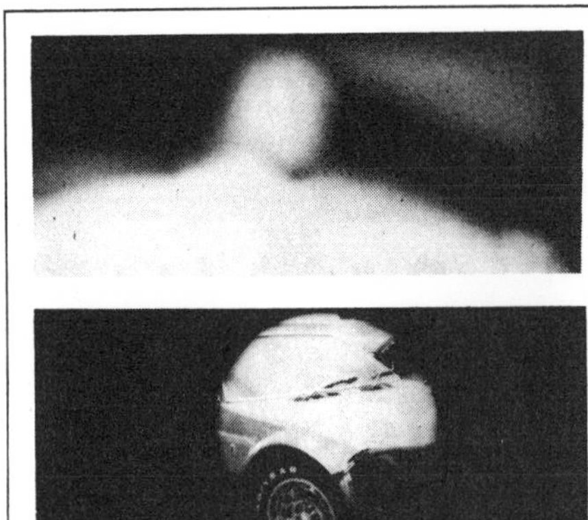

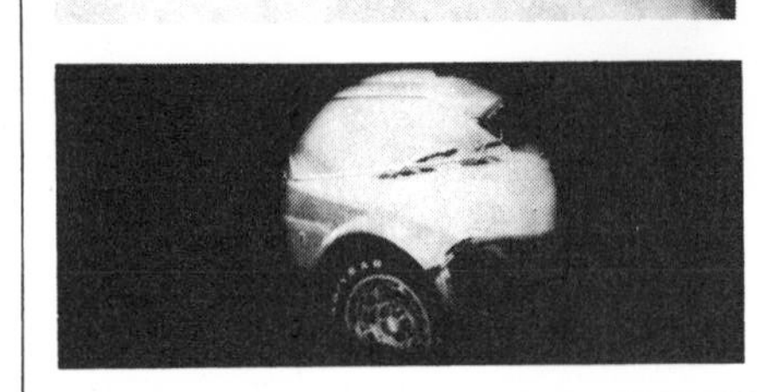

(Top) What Bill sees; what Sally sees. *(Bottom)* Tunnel vision; glaucoma causes this vision.

invited me to a special sports meet there. The games and contests were set up so that a person's disability didn't make any difference. Kids in wheelchairs were racing each other, competing in archery and shot put, and playing basketball on teams. There were obstacle relays for kids in braces and with crutches. Some of those kids could do fantastic things.

Marielle has cerebral palsy. When she was born, something injured the part of her brain that controls the movement of her muscles. Her brain sends her muscles signals to bend, even when Marielle doesn't want them to. Because of that, her movements are shaky and jerky. Her speech is hard to understand because the muscles in her jaw are affected. It takes a lot of effort for Marielle to walk and talk and move the way *she* wants to. It's a good thing cerebral palsy isn't painful. It's sure inconvenient, though.

Marielle spends part of every day in *physical therapy*. She does special exercises that help her muscles to relax and to grow stronger. It can be hard work.

Another kind of orthopedic handicap happens when you lose a part of your body, like an arm or a leg. I don't think I would call Andre "handicapped," however. Nothing stops *him* from anything!

Andre lost the bottom part of his leg, just below the knee, after a bicycle accident. Andre himself helped make the decision to have the leg amputated when it became necessary. Now he has an artificial leg made of rubber and plastic.

An artificial body part is called a *prosthesis.* Andre's been using prostheses since he was five years old. As he gets bigger, he gets new ones that fit the new size. His prosthesis doesn't do any fancy tricks like the Bionic Man, but Andre can do just about anything else. Sometimes he turns the foot around and walks into class backward!

It can be hard getting used to not having a part of your body. Some people feel ashamed of themselves at first. Why should they? They're still the same *inside* as they used to be. After all, when it comes to what you like in a person, that's what's most important.

Once a guy at McDonald's asked me about my braces; I was glad. When he understood he didn't think it was anything weird. Maybe he guessed that it's better to ask politely about a person's disability than to keep silent and come to the wrong conclusion. Maybe he knew that I'm just myself—Jed—and I've got a certain kind of problem that I've got to deal with. I just happen to talk a little better than I walk. It could have been the other way around. So what!

My name is Toni.

I like rock music, and dancing and reading historical novels. And I have lots of pets—two dogs, a rabbit, two hamsters, and a couple of turtles. Maybe you can't tell from the pictures, but if we met in person you'd probably notice right away that I'm blind. You'd know by my cane, and by my eyes.

I know many people feel funny about meeting a blind person. That's probably the worst thing about having a handicap—the way it affects other people's reaction to you.

I'm in the eighth grade now, and I've been going to classes in a regular junior high for the past three years. At first it was really scary being with regular kids because I'd been at a school where all the kids had problems like mine. But after everybody got used to me and I got used to them, I started to love regular school. Having friends who understand makes all the difference in the world. It makes you feel free.

My old school was a special school for blind kids (we usually use the more modern term *visually handicapped* or *VH*). That's where I learned *Braille,* a system of writing that uses raised dots, like bumps, on the paper. I read by feeling the bumps. I write by typing them on a machine called a *Braillewriter.* I can also use a regular typewriter.

I still go back to my old school for extra help and for special events. When people first see a group of kids like those at my old school, they usually think of helplessness and of being totally in the dark. But it's not like that. There are different kinds of visual handicaps and different degrees of blindness.

The law says that a person is *legally blind* if she or he has 20:200 vision or less in the better eye while using glasses or contact lenses. That means the person can see something from 20 feet away that a normally sighted person can see from 200 feet.

Blind people prefer to hold a friend's elbow when crossing streets.

"Fill? I thought he said *spill*!"

However, the legally blind person probably won't see it clearly.

Bill, who is legally blind, might see light-colored shadows and outlines.

What Sally sees is more like what you see when it's dark.

Sometimes a person sees only the center part of what others see. That's called *tunnel vision.*

Losing sight in the *center* is a symptom of *glaucoma,* the most common eye disease.

Nearsightedness and *farsightedness* are usually less serious problems and easy to correct with glasses or contacts. A *far*sighted person sees *distant* things clearly, but something close is blurred. *Near*sightedness is just the opposite.

Totally blind probably sounds terrible to a seeing person, but it isn't. I was born without sight, so I don't miss it as much as you might think I would. Without sight there are still music and sounds, friends to talk to, fragrances, and how things feel when you touch them. There's thinking and daydreaming, physical activities, and all the various emotions. It's a full life. With so much going on, I don't have time to be very sad about something I haven't ever experienced.

What's bad is when people feel so sorry for us that we start to feel sorry for ourselves. It's especially hard when we get left out of things because someone believes we can't understand what's happening.

With special training even a totally blind person can do quite a lot. When I walk down the street, I swing my white cane along the ground in front of me to find out if there is anything in my way. I also listen carefully for clues that give me information, such as traffic noises and familiar sounds.

Learning to get around is called *orientation and mobility training.* Instead of canes, some people have dog guides. However, you must still know how to get where you're going whenever you go to a new place. The dog doesn't *take* you there. It just lets you know where walls and doors and obstacles are located, much like the way the cane does.

In learning mobility, you start by feeling. You protect yourself from bumping into things by holding your arms in front of your body. One arm protects your chest and face; the other, your stomach and thighs. This method of travel is called *trailing.* It's mostly for little kids.

When you get older, you learn to use the cane or a dog. You memorize where many things are, especially at home and at school and at other important places. It requires concentration and paying attention all the time. Maybe that's one reason kids sometimes think I'm so serious—because I'm concentrating.

Once in a while, somebody comes along and asks if I want help crossing the street. I appreciate their thoughtfulness. Of course, like anyone else, I have to be careful about strangers. When I'm crossing the street with a person, or walking with a friend in an unfamiliar place, I like to use the standard method that all VH people use. I hold her or his arm just above the elbow. I can follow really well that way, and it's a nice way to travel.

I love to go to the shopping center, but buying clothes can be a problem. Since I can't tell what color something is, my friends help me pick out my clothes. When I get home, I make Braille labels for things that feel similar but are different colors, such as jeans and T-shirts. With the labels to tell me the colors, I can get dressed without asking for help.

Other aids that people with visual handicaps use in learning, working, and playing include books with large print, hand-held magnifiers, TV-screen magnifiers, special systems and rules in games and sports, talking computers, and records and tapes.

There are records that are called *talking books;* they contain the reading of an entire book but speeded up to go faster than normal speech. I know how to listen very quickly!

The high school I'm going to next year is a regular high school. It has a room with all the special equipment I might need to keep up with my schoolwork, such as textbooks in Braille and on tape, and a teacher to help and advise me. I'll go there when I need to between my regular classes.

There's one thing I still want to know more about and I hope my friends will help me, because it's important and I can't learn it by myself. It's how to come off okay around other people—you know, how to be popular and "in" on things. I suppose everybody spends some time trying to figure that out. Handicapped kids, though, might need extra help. For instance, VH kids sometimes forget to hold their heads up. Sometimes they're ashamed of how their eyes look. Well, they have to get over that. A friend can remind them to look up by saying, "I'm over here. Look at me."

By the way, don't be afraid to use words like "look" or "see." It doesn't embarrass us. In fact, it's embarrassing when people try to avoid those words, because it can't be done. Besides, we have a good idea of what those words mean. We use them, too.

I like to be treated the same as everybody else, as far as possible, and that's pretty far! →

My name is Matt Ward.

I have a learning disability.

Some kids seem to be terrific at schoolwork without even trying. Me, I really work hard just to keep up. I figure it's a job that I do because I have to. I want to be a doctor some day, so I've got to keep on top of it.

They say that the brain is like a complicated computer. If that's so, then my wires are a little crossed up. For instance, I'm right-handed on some things and left-handed on others. And I often get mixed up over which is which.

My memory plays tricks on me, too, and causes two big school problems. One is that I have trouble remembering what letters *sound* like when they're put together. I'm *always* forgetting what happens when "A" and "E" are together. Sometimes the word "neat" seems as though it's really two words—"ne at." Sometimes I think it's "net," or "nate," as if it rhymed with "great" And sometimes I can remember that it's "neat." That slows down my reading because I know there wouldn't be a sentence that says, "He was ne at in his work," so I know I have to stop and check it out again.

The other problem is that I can easily forget how a word is supposed to *look*. If I copy it from a book, I get it right. But when I'm on my own, especially in reading, I sometimes goof up. The word "great" might come out "gneat" because "r" often looks like "n" to me. You'd get stuck, too, if you were trying to read a word like "gneat." I guess I look at the lines too much, and not enough at the spaces. They call that a *perceptual* handicap.

I even write backward if I'm not careful. Other people have to work hard to do that. For me, it just happens. They don't know why my brain turns things around. I'm not slow at understanding, and I can solve hard problems. But somehow, after the information gets inside my head, it becomes a little jumbled.

During summer, my brother Jim and I take turns working at our dad's gas station. That job is easy for me, but there are people with other kinds of learning disabilities who're just as smart as I am but who might have trouble with it.

One type of learning disability is not being able to sit or stand still. You're all over the place, making everybody nervous. Luckily, most kids outgrow being *hyperactive.*

Another problem is having *poor eye-hand coordination.* This can cause trouble with handwriting and with certain sports. A person with this problem might bang up the side of a car trying to get the gas nozzle into the tank. If the car got scratched, the owner would probably be upset.

Judging distance can be difficult for some people. They're not good at putting objects into the right places. Other people have trouble organizing mathematics on paper. If the numbers are not in the proper column, you can't add them up correctly. A person like that wouldn't do well making out a customer's bill.

Some people *perseverate.* That means that it's very difficult for them to change from one activity to another. A person who's perseverating might clean a windshield three times and not notice that the customer was getting impatient to leave.

Anomia interferes with a person expressing what's on her or his mind. For example, the attendant *knows* that the car needs a new fan belt but just can't think of the *word* for it. "We've got to change the . . . the . . . um . . . that rubber thing." Anomia happens to everybody once in a while. If it happens a lot, it becomes a learning disability.

Some learning-disabled kids have difficulty with spoken words. The sound gets *in,* but then it doesn't register right. It's like the time Jim asked me to fill the water bucket, and I thought he said *spill* it.

You can imagine how annoying it could be to have a handicap like one of those. When my mom first noticed *I* was having trouble, she took me to a child development clinic to see what was going on. They gave me a lot of tests, physical and mental, and they told us that there's at least one person in almost every classroom who has some kind of learning disability. Often you can barely notice it. My problem is pretty common. In fact, so common that many schools have special materials and special programs to help kids like me. They teach us to focus on the details that give us trouble. Sometimes the doctor will prescribe a special diet or medication, since it's really a *physical* problem. And the teacher may even change the way she tests so that the student has a better chance to show what she or he understands.

Of course, not all learning problems are learning disabilities. If you miss a lot of school, you'll get behind. If you don't pay attention in class, you'll miss information that you need. If the language you speak at school is different from the one you use at home, you might get confused. However, those things are not learning disabilities. They are not a result of something not working quite right in your brain.

I think the worst part of my learning disability is that I get awfully tired of goofing up and looking like a failure. Even though I understand what my problem is, it's hard. I get so angry at myself sometimes that I feel like crying. When that happens, I try to get away alone for a while.

Jim's a "normie" . . . he doesn't have any kind of disability, so far as I can tell. He says he sometimes wishes he had mine, so he'd have an excuse when he makes mistakes. That's one thing I'd catch it for from my folks—making phony excuses.

I don't have to be perfect, but when it comes to school, I have to give it my best shot. It's the only way to go.

Barbara Adams, a film maker, specializes in producing media for rehabilitation and special education. She holds a master's degree in rehabilitation counseling.

STORIES FOR FREE CHILDREN

A Few Cents More

By Sara D. Kash
Illustrated by Carol Gillot

Noah and Michael had been friends for as far back as they could remember. They were both seven years old, they were in the same class, they played together after supper every day, and Noah's mother and Michael's father worked side by side on the assembly line at the factory in town.

Noah and his mother lived in an apartment just down the street from the house that Michael lived in with his parents and his sister. (Noah's parents were divorced, and his father lived in another city with his new wife.)

Noah and his mother would often leave the house together in the morning. They would walk together as far as the school bus stop. In the afternoon Noah always got home before his mother.

But one day, Noah was very surprised to find his mother there when he opened the door.

"Why are you home so early?" Noah asked.

"I left early because I was upset about something that happened at work," she said, tears filling her eyes. Noah had hardly ever seen her cry.

"You always make me tell you what's wrong when I'm upset," he said.

Noah's mother breathed a big sigh and took his hand. "I found out at work today that Michael's father makes more money than I do."

Noah waited for her to go on with the story, but she stopped.

"I don't understand, Mom."

"Michael's father and I have been at the factory for the same number of years; we both do exactly the same job; and he gets fifty cents more an hour than I do," she explained. "Do you think that's fair?"

Noah thought hard for a minute. He really couldn't see anything fair

about it at all. "Why don't you just ask your boss for more money?" he said.

"I just had my yearly raise," his mother replied, "and I still make less than Michael's father. I'm really mad about this, Noah, and I intend to do something about it! I'll talk to my boss first thing tomorrow." She kissed Noah on the forehead and went into the kitchen.

After dinner Noah went over to Michael's house to play board games. Michael's father had already told him about what had happened at work that day. "My dad says that he *should* be making more because he is a man and he has a family to support," Michael told Noah.

"But, my mom has to take care of me without any help," Noah said. "I think she needs the money just as bad as your dad."

"Well, your mom should be home," said Michael. "My mom is always here when we get home from school."

Noah thought about all the days his mother had to work late and he had to wait alone in the apartment. Tears started to burn his eyes. "My mom can't stay home because we need the money she earns," Noah yelled. He threw the game board across the room. "I'm going home. I hate you, and I hate your father."

Noah went straight to bed that night, and in the morning, he left for school earlier than usual. When his mother came home that afternoon, Noah asked her what had happened at work when she talked to her boss.

"He won't do anything. He told me I do good work and he would hate to see me leave just for a few cents more an hour." Noah's mother laughed. "A few cents more! Do you know what I can do with those few cents more!"

Noah remembered all the things he'd had to give up because they didn't have quite enough money. He started to feel almost as angry as his mother.

"What will you do now?" he asked.

"I could forget it, but *somebody* has to fight when things are so unfair," she answered. "I know there are other women at work who are getting less money than the men they work with.

I'm going to talk with them, and maybe we can get together to do something about this discrimination."

Noah remembered having heard that word a lot of times on the news and in school. His teacher told the class about people doing it to other people because of their color.

"Isn't discrimination treating people unfairly because of the color of their skin?" he asked his mother.

"Discrimination can happen for a lot of reasons," she said. "Michael's father and I should be treated just alike—because we do the same work equally well—but he is treated better just because he is a man."

At that moment, the doorbell rang and outside stood Michael and his father.

"I really think you're making a big deal out of this whole thing," Michael's father told Noah's mother. "Now it's affecting our boys' friendship. Do you think that's right?"

Noah's mother's face was sad. "No, I don't think it's right that our boys have to fight over our problem, but I also don't think it's right that you make more than I do, and I intend to do something about it."

"You could lose your job over this," Michael's father said.

When Noah heard those words, he felt really scared. What if his mother did lose her job? Would she be able to get another one? Maybe she should forget the whole thing and just go back to work. Noah looked at Michael and he remembered the things Michael said about his father needing more money because he was a man. Noah became more and more angry.

"My mom's going to make this right," he heard himself saying. "This is discrimination."

Michael's father got up to leave. "I guess that's where it stands," he said sternly. "I'll see you tomorrow."

After they left, Noah's mother bent down and hugged him. "I'm so proud of you," she said.

Early that week Michael and Noah stayed away from each other in school, but by Thursday they were passing notes back and forth, and by Friday, they were walking home together. Neither of them said he was sorry, but both of them had silently decided they were still friends.

Friday night Michael slept overnight at Noah's. Saturday morning, Noah's mother went out shopping before the boys woke. When she returned, she handed each of the boys a colored cap. She gave the red one to Michael and the green one to Noah. At breakfast, they sat in their pajamas with their caps on.

"Would you boys help me out today?" she asked. "There are some heavy boxes I want taken down to the storage room. Since it's really hard work, I'll even pay you for doing it. How does that sound?"

Michael and Noah were excited. They started talking about how they would spend the money.

The boys worked all afternoon. Some of the boxes had dishes and glasses in them and they were really heavy. Some contained just papers and clothing, and they were lighter. Noah and Michael took turns carrying light and heavy boxes. At three o'clock they finished the job. They were tired and covered with dust and dirt.

"Well, I suppose you want your money," said Noah's mother, reaching for her purse. "Here's three dollars for you," she said handing some money to Noah. "And here's two dollars for you, Michael."

Michael looked at the money. "Hey, why is he getting more than me?" he asked. "Oh," said Noah's mother. "Don't you know that boys with green caps *always* get more than boys with red caps."

Michael thought she was joking, but from the look on her face, he could tell she wasn't.

"That's wrong," he said. "We did the same work. I worked just as hard and just as long as Noah did. Either Noah should get two dollars or I should get three dollars."

"Sorry," said Noah's mother. "It may seem unfair, but that's how it is."

"I'm going home," shouted Michael, slamming the door behind him as he left.

"Do you know why I did that to Michael?" his mother asked.

"You did it to show Michael that when two people do the same job they should get the same money."

"That's right," said his mother. "And I'm sure Michael will be back."

Within ten minutes the doorbell rang. Noah let in Michael wearing his red cap and his father wearing a frown. "I think we should have a talk," said Michael's father.

"Michael told me what you did this afternoon, and he asked me why," Michael's father said to Noah's mother. "I'm afraid I didn't have a good answer for him, and I guess I don't have a good answer for why I should be making more money than you do on the job. I want my boy to learn what fairness is, and I guess I'm not setting a good example. I want to apologize. . . and I want you to know that I plan to help you do whatever you have to do to make things right at work. You can count on me."

Noah's mother's mouth turned upward into a big smile. "I'm so pleased you said that. On Monday we women will have another meeting with the boss and we may need your help to argue for our rights. In the meantime, I think I owe Michael a dollar."

Michael's father laughed. "Let's have ice cream cones to celebrate," he said. "My treat."

Noah and Michael hugged each other. "Dad, can I have a double scoop?" Michael asked.

"Can everyone wearing red or green caps have a double scoop?" asked Noah.

And the four of them laughed all the way to the ice cream store.

Sara D. Kash, a former teacher, is now a financial analyst in Rochester, New York. This is her first published story.

There are many kinds of guns. One kind is called a pistol. Or a rod. Police officers carry it. So do crooks. It kills people. Last year, in accidents and in crimes, all types of guns killed 30,000 children, women, and men in the United States. The U.S. murder rate alone was more than the total of gun deaths in Western Europe, Canada, Mexico, and Japan put together.

Another gun is called a rifle. (See page 106) Soldiers carry it. So do hunters. It kills people and animals, too.

Soldiers also use a gun called a submachine gun. (See page 104) So do gangsters; in movies they sometimes carry this gun in violin cases. It shoots lots and lots of bullets, fast, so it can kill lots and lots of people at one time.

There are many other kinds of guns. Double-barreled shotguns and sawed-off shotguns can shoot a lot of small lead pieces that spray over a much larger area than bullets of other guns. Antique guns are guns that some people like to collect and display in their houses. All guns have one thing in common. They kill living things.

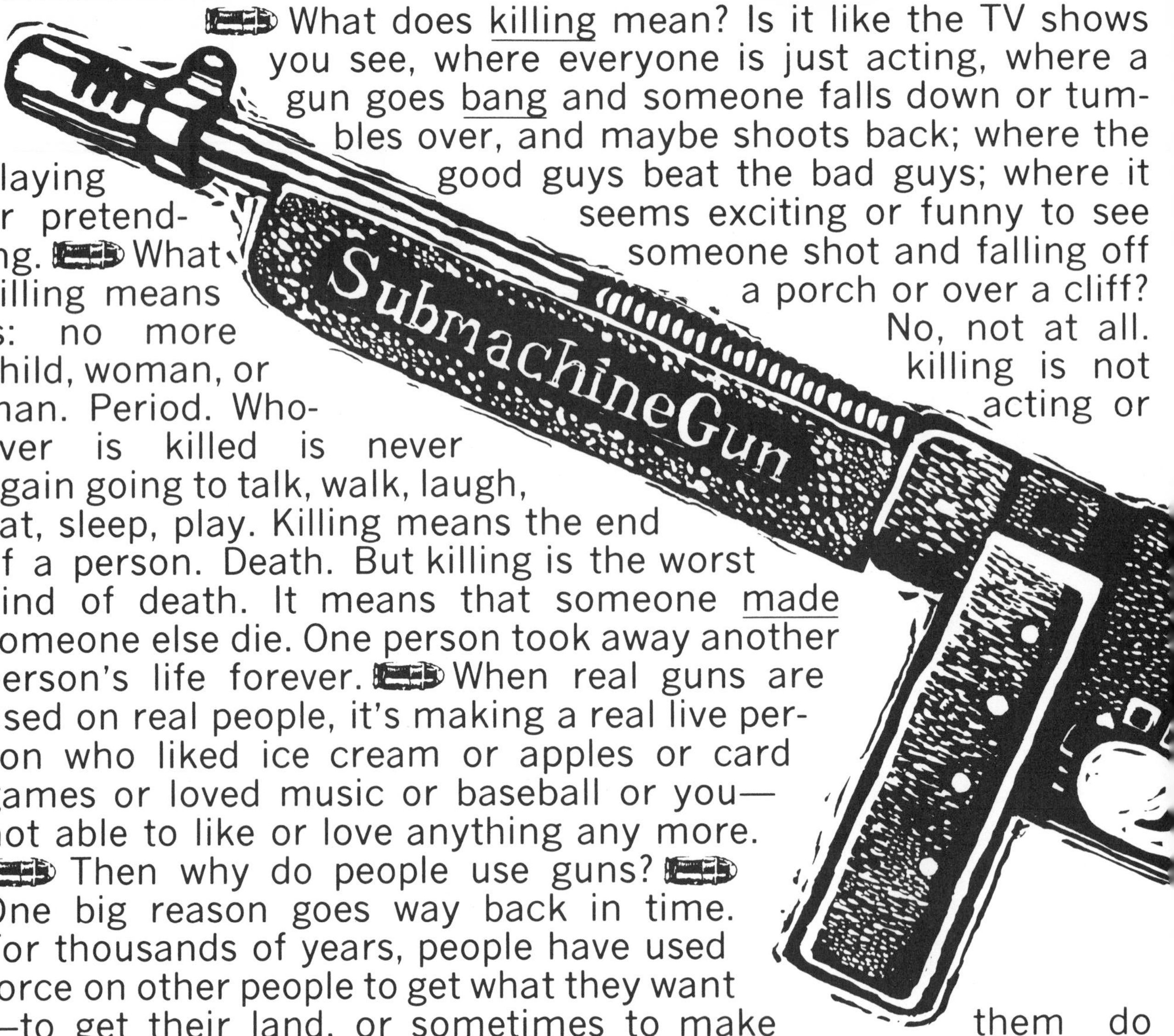

What does *killing* mean? Is it like the TV shows you see, where everyone is just acting, where a gun goes *bang* and someone falls down or tumbles over, and maybe shoots back; where the good guys beat the bad guys; where it seems exciting or funny to see someone shot and falling off a porch or over a cliff? No, not at all. killing is not acting or playing or pretending. What killing means is: no more child, woman, or man. Period. Whoever is killed is never again going to talk, walk, laugh, eat, sleep, play. Killing means the end of a person. Death. But killing is the worst kind of death. It means that someone *made* someone else die. One person took away another person's life forever. When real guns are used on real people, it's making a real live person who liked ice cream or apples or card games or loved music or baseball or you—not able to like or love anything any more. Then why do people use guns? One big reason goes way back in time. For thousands of years, people have used force on other people to get what they want—to get their land, or sometimes to make them do their work. Slavery came about this way. There once were slaves in the United States. Today, there are people who are not slaves but who live in constant fear of their country's military police. Another big reason why people use guns is that some people think guns will make them be "Big Shots." They think that fighting with guns helps them show courage and will make them heroes. Some people are ready to hurt others while in the act of stealing money or stealing land. But do guns help prevent attacks from these kinds of people? Maybe. Sometimes. But there are also times when innocent people die just because someone had a gun and pulled the trigger too quickly or carelessly. Even when guns aren't used for fighting or war or stealing, people like to show off their guns by marching with them in parades. In some countries big cannons and big tanks with big guns are part of the parade, too. All these war machines are supposed to make people who feel small and unimportant feel bigger and more important than everyone else. Guns are also used in salutes. When a famous person comes to visit a country or when someone special dies, shooting off a lot of guns is thought to be a way of honoring that person. (Usually he or she is a king or queen, or the president of a country.) Would you consider it an honor to hear big guns make a big bang for you? No one would honor a great painter or doctor or writer or botanist with guns, would they? Long ago in America (and today in some parts of the world), guns were used to hunt for food. There were no butcher shops or supermarkets, and people had to shoot animals to get meat for dinner. After all, people get hungry and people do eat animals. But even though we no longer hunt for our food, some people still like to see how good their aim is. They say animals don't have the same feelings that people do. Nowadays when animals are killed to make meat, they are slaughtered by experts who do it quickly and painlessly. People who feel small inside think they are bigger because they killed a deer or an elephant. But shooting animals can be cruel even if they don't get killed. They may be injured and have to live in pain. Another reason some people argue for guns is that there are people who make money from manufacturing and selling guns. Piles and piles of money. Some companies have been making different types of guns for years and years. Other companies make money by selling bullets and gunpowder; others print books and catalogs about guns; others mail and ship guns; others make movies about guns and fighting.

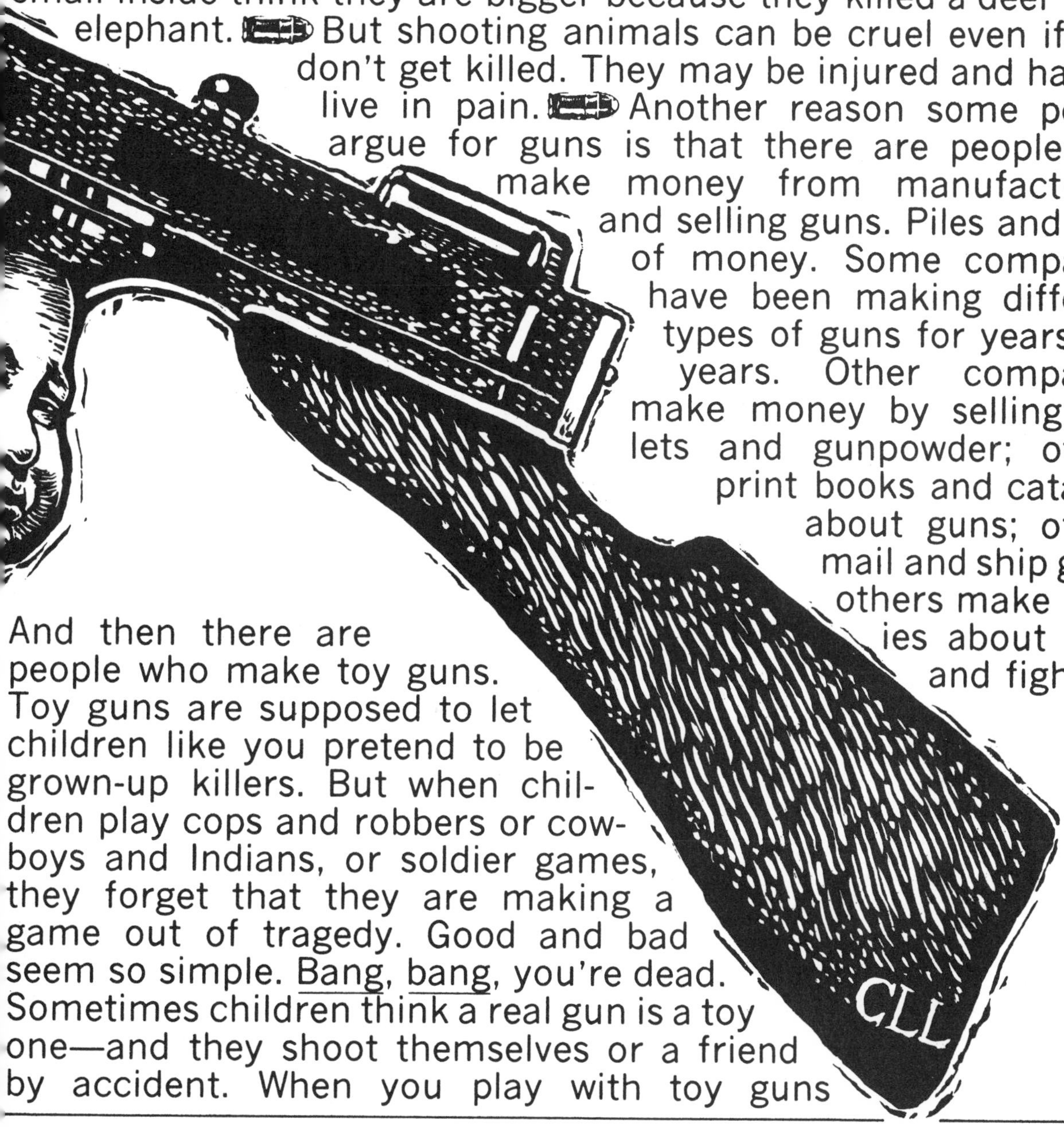

And then there are people who make toy guns. Toy guns are supposed to let children like you pretend to be grown-up killers. But when children play cops and robbers or cowboys and Indians, or soldier games, they forget that they are making a game out of tragedy. Good and bad seem so simple. Bang, bang, you're dead. Sometimes children think a real gun is a toy one—and they shoot themselves or a friend by accident. When you play with toy guns throughout your childhood, you and other children get used to thinking that guns are okay, that being fierce is better than being kind and gentle. And it isn't.

Hasn't anyone thought of limiting the use of guns? Yes, some men and women have tried for many years to get the use of guns under strict control. And lots of people have tried to stop toy companies from making and selling toy guns. Many teachers, parents, ministers, priests, rabbis, legislators, poets, doctors, lawyers have talked against guns. But the people who make and sell guns want to continue making money, and the people who like to use guns fight against gun-control laws. Some of these gun-lovers even think that children should be trained to use guns the right way.

There is no right way to use a gun. A gun always means hurting or killing a person or an animal. Some people say they use guns to learn how to hit a mark. (They can practice in a shooting gallery.) What does anyone need to shoot straight <u>for</u>, anyway?

Finally, some people say that <u>at least</u> police officers and soldiers need to use guns. This may be true in the United States. But it doesn't have to be. In England, the local police only carry guns once in a great while. And English people still do not kill as often as people kill each other in our country.

Soldiers? Well, maybe if nobody used guns, we wouldn't need soldiers. How can killing solve big problems? You get rid of some soldiers, but more always take their place. And the big problem doesn't really go away until people talk about their differences.

Maybe if children all over the world stopped playing with guns, maybe there wouldn't be any killing or any need for soldiers when you grow up. Maybe, if you and your friends tried to settle your differences by talking and by convincing the other person of your point of view, maybe we'll get rid of the idea that violence ever solves problems or changes people's minds.

And maybe if you, just you alone, begin to think about what guns really mean, and see that the shine and polish and big noise and games and parades and salutes all hide what guns are for—maybe then we'll start to save the lives of people right where you live, <u>and</u> all over the world.

You can refuse to play with toy guns. You can also tell the government how you feel about controlling the use of real guns. Write a letter today to Representative John Conyers, U.S. Congress, Washington, D.C. 20515. Your opinion counts!

Shirley Camper Soman is a social worker, writer, lecturer and crusader against violence.

Stories For Free Children ©

is that your sister?

My name is Catherine. I am six years old. And I am adopted.

I have a sister who is four years old and she is adopted, too. Kids at school or in the park are always asking me, "Is that your *sister*?" Sometimes when they see my mother, the kids ask, "Is that your *mother*?" I know they ask these questions because my sister and my mother and I don't look anything alike. We don't have the same kind of skin or face or hair. I tell the kids that my sister and I are adopted. Then they ask me, "What's adopted?"

It makes me feel good to know something the other kids don't know. My friend Melissa knows because she is adopted, too. I don't think she has to explain all the time the way I do because she has blond hair just like her mother. They look a lot alike.

I try to tell the kids everything I know about adoption, but the more things I try to explain to them, the more things I think of to ask my mother. Like I'll say to some kids, "Well, it's like this. A woman born me, but she couldn't keep me and my mommy and daddy wanted me, so they adopted me."

After I tell them that, I ask my mommy, "Why couldn't that woman who born me keep me. Didn't she like me?"

My mommy says, "You were just born. She didn't have time to know you and love you. You were very little when she decided to allow your adoption."

Sometimes I want to hear more than just that, and I say, "But why did she *allow* my adoption?" Well, my mommy tries not to lie to me so I'm not surprised when she says, "I don't know. I don't know enough about the woman to know what went on in her mind." Then Mommy will say, "What do you think?"

One time I said, "she was a nice lady who was very, very poor. She had no money for food and she wore a sweater with big holes." Another time I said she was young with long hair she wore in a ponytail. I wear a ponytail sometimes. Sometimes I get sad and all mixed up thinking about her.

We can talk like that for a long time until Mommy says, "It's nice to daydream, but I do know that the woman knew she couldn't go about the serious business of taking care of a child. Not every woman who bears a child can do it, for one reason or another. We can only guess at what her reason may have been."

a true story of adoption by Catherine and Sherry Bunin →

Carla + Me in Front of Alec's Beach

Me + Daddy

My Brothers, Carla + Me

That's what I end up telling kids about the woman who born me. I say, "Well, she just couldn't cope, I guess."

When we get that out of the way, kids want to know where my mommy and daddy found me. I think they believe those stories about babies being left in baskets on people's doorsteps and about lost little kids being taken in by some good people who give them good food to eat. I don't think things like that really happen. I tell them that most kids get adopted from an adoption agency.

I was too little to remember my adoption agency, but I went to see the agency where my sister, Carla, came from. It was a nice building with offices and typewriters and a water tank with paper cups on the side that anyone could take if they were thirsty. It looked a little like my daddy's office, but here they take care of the business of kids. We didn't see any kids because kids don't live at the agency. Sometimes they come to visit the way Carla and I did, but kids who haven't been adopted live in foster homes or in other places somewhere.

"What's a foster home?" some kid is sure to ask me. And I tell them that a foster home is a home with a family who takes care of kids until they have a family of their own. Some kids have to stay a long, long time. I didn't. I don't remember my foster family because I was only three months when I was adopted. Some kids aren't so lucky. They get tired of waiting for a family to come along. Even if they like the foster people, kids want their own family, a forever family.

My sister Carla remembers her foster family very well. She was just about three years old when she came to live with us. In fact, she thinks her foster mother was the woman who born her, bu that's not true. I'll explain it to her better when she gets bigger.

After all the talking and explaining I do, someone will always say, "Yeah, but don't you know who your *real* mom and dad are?" I tell them that my *real* mom and dad are the mom and dad who take care of me and love me. But no matter how I try, I can't seem to explain that very well. I don't know why.

Most grown-ups don't know any more about adoption than kids and they ask me the same dumb questions. It makes me wish my mommy *had* born me and that I looked just like her. When I tell Mommy this, she says, "Thata's a beautiful thing to say because that means that you love me." Then she explains how, when I grow up, I'll learn to make use of everything about me that is me and I'll be "a beautiful human being." She thinks I'm going to be the first woman President of the United States or someone even better. She can get all excited thinking about me grown-up.

Most of the time I'm glad I was adopted.

My mommy and daddy already had two kids when they adopted me. They could have had more kids, I know, but they knew that there were plenty of kids like Carla and me who wanted a family and they wanted more kids, so it seemed like a good idea for all of us to get together. That's why they went to the adoption agency.

Do you know what the person who works at the agency to bring families together is called? A social worker. I don't remember my social worker at my agency, but I met Carla's social worker lots of times.

When she first came to our house, she talked to us kids in the family. She asked us if we'd like to have another kid around.

I told the social worker I wanted a sister because there were two boys in the family and there should be two girls, not just one, me. Then I showed the social worker where my sister would sleep. In my room, in a double-decker bed. She'd sleep in the down bunk and I'd sleep in the up bunk. It was a nice visit, but Mommy bit her fingernails the whole time.

The next visit was the best. Two social workers came and they brought Carla for her first visit.

Nicholas + Me

Me + Everybody

Me + the Family

Carla was real little, with skinny legs. She looked like a doll. Mommy and Daddy had already met her and they were right—all us kids liked her right away.

They came again in a couple of days and this time they brought Carla along to stay with us for good. They brought her clothes and a couple of old toys, and you know what else? Her baby blanket. That little kid loved to hold that blanket and put her finger in her mouth. Me and my brothers made her laugh when we put our fingers in our mouths to show her how she looked.

When Carla first came, she couldn't talk, but now she talks more than I do.

After Carla first came to stay, the social worker made a couple more visits to see how the family was doing and then Mommy and Daddy and the social worker began talking about going to court. At first I thought that meant a court with a judge and a jury and good and bad lawyers and things like that. I was scared a bad lawyer would take Carla away. Mommy explained that no kids are adopted until they have lived with a family for six months. Then the family goes to before a judge and swears they want that kid to stay in the family forever.

I try and try to remember when I went to court. Mommy says it wasn't a court at all. I sat in the judge's office while she and Daddy raised their hands and swore they'd take good care of me. Then I was made lawfully their daughter. Aferwards, we had a big celebration. I sure wish I could remember.

We went to court with Carla in the morning and we were almost late because we couldn't find a taxi big enough to take all of us. Finally we got a nice taxi driver who let us sit on each other's laps. When we got to Family Court a big man came out into the hall and told us to follow him and he took us into an office with a desk and couch and a few chairs. Behind the desk sat a judge. She shook everybody's hand, and she seemed glad to see us. There sure were a lot of papers. My mommy looked like she was crying and so did the social workers, but I just wanted the judge to hurry and get it all over with. Carla's shoes were all over my dress because she was moving around so much. That judge took her time, though. I guess she wanted to make sure we all knew what we were getting into and that Carla would be in our family forever and ever.

When we left, we went right to a big celebration lunch and we all got to order anything we wanted, which meant millions of French fries.

When I think about it now, it was really nice.

Now, that is all I know about adoption. I don't think about it much unless someone starts asking me questions. I don't think Carla thanks much about it either. Neither do our brothers. We are The Family. We fight a lot just like all the families I know. We fight about television and who gets the most cookies.

Mommy yells at all of us, and sometimes Daddy brings us ice cream sandwiches when he does the shopping on Saturday.

We don't have much time to think about this adoption business. But when we ride the subway or bus, people stare at us. And when we go to restaurants people look at us too. They look at us nicely. I don't care if they look. I really like it.

And that's all there is to it. You know what makes me laugh sometimes when I tell my story? Kids. Some of them will always say they wish someone could adopt them. Some of the kids say they think they *are* adopted, but their parents won't tell them. Thoses kids probably aren't adopted at all. My mom and dad say parents should be honest with their kids and it wouldn't be honest if they didn't tell them.

So that's my story.

Catherine Bunin lives in New York City with her parents, her sister, and her brothers, Alexander and Nicholas. Sherry Bunin, is a free-lance writer.

Charlie Helps

By Nancy McArthur
Illustrations by
Robbin Schiff

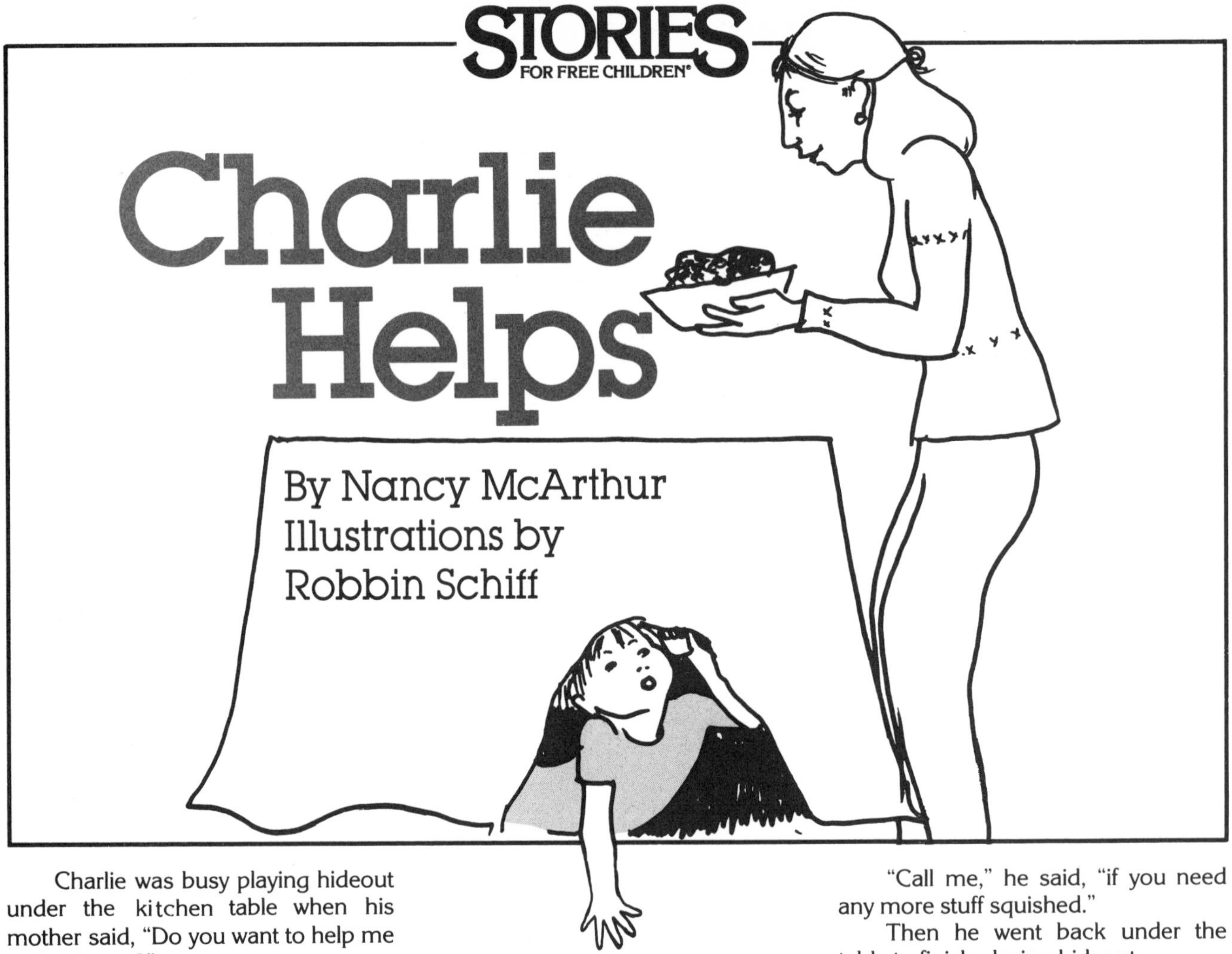

Charlie was busy playing hideout under the kitchen table when his mother said, "Do you want to help me make dinner?"

"I don't know how to do that," said Charlie, sticking his head out from under the tablecloth to see what was going on.

"You can make the hamburgers," she said.

"I don't know how to do that either," he answered.

"I'll show you," she said. "You just have to squish them flat."

"I like to squish things," said Charlie. "Clay and mud and stuff."

"First go and wash your hands really clean."

He went to the bathroom sink and soaped up his hands. Then he wiped them carefully until all the dirt came off on the towel.

"I'm ready," he told his mother.

She put a pile of pink ground meat in front of him. "Now," she instructed, "take a bunch of meat and make a ball out of it."

He did that.

"You need a little more meat," she said. "Wait, that's too much. Take a little off. There. That's just right. Now put the palm of your hand on the ball of meat. Ready! Set! Squish!"

Charlie squished.

"Not too flat," she said. "That's enough. Good. You've just made a hamburger."

"I want to make another one," he said.

"We need three more," his mother told him. When he got through, she said, "You're a very good hamburger-squisher."

"Call me," he said, "if you need any more stuff squished."

Then he went back under the table to finish playing hideout.

At dinner Charlie thought his hamburger was extra especially good because he had squished it himself.

Charlie was busy thinking one day when his mother said, "I need your help. Please come and play with Chrissie. She won't go to sleep and she keeps crying every time I go out of the room."

Charlie didn't like to play with his baby sister.

"Why doesn't she be quiet?" he asked.

"She wants some attention," his mother explained. "Everybody needs a lot of that. Come and play with her for a while."

"I don't want to," said Charlie.

"Please help me with this," she said. "I'm so tired and I want to lie down and rest a while."

"Okay," said Charlie, even though he didn't want to.

His mother gave him a hug.

Chrissie was in her playpen. She was crying and whining and rattling the bars.

"Be quiet," said Charlie.

She went right on crying.

Charlie picked up her stuffed bear from the floor and gave it to her.

Chrissie threw it back on the floor.

Charlie went and got his cowboy hat. "Look, I'm a cowboy," he said and galloped around the room.

Chrissie started crying slower and slower. Pretty soon she wasn't crying at all. She was watching Charlie gallop around the room.

When he got tired of galloping, he switched to hopping.

"Now I'm a frog. See me hopping? I'm a cowboy frog."

Chrissie smiled at him.

"When you get bigger," he said, "I'll teach you how to be a frog. And a cowboy, too."

She was looking sleepy.

Charlie patted her soft little hand.

"Sometimes," he told her, "you make me mad, but sometimes I like you anyway."

He patted her some more. Then he hummed for a long time. First he hummed "Jingle Bells." Then "Mary Had a Little Lamb." When he couldn't think of any more songs, he made some up.

Chrissie fell asleep.

Charlie tiptoed into his mother's room.

He whispered, "Mom, are you asleep."

"Yes," she said. She opened one eye. "Is Chrissie asleep?"

"Yeah," said Charlie. "I galloped and hopped and hummed for her and she went to sleep."

"Thank you," said his mother with both her eyes closed. "I don't know what I'd do without you."

Charlie was busy kicking a stone along the sidewalk one day when his mother called him to come inside right that minute.

She said, "You've got to clean up this mess."

"What mess?" said Charlie, even though he already knew.

"All these toys and things of yours you've left all over the floor and every-place else. People can't walk around in here."

"I can," said Charlie.

"Never mind," she said. "You made this mess. So it's your job to clean it up."

"I don't want to," said Charlie. "I hate cleaning up."

"I hate cleaning up, too," said his mother. "Nobody likes it. But it has to be done."

"Why?" asked Charlie because he didn't want to do it and sometimes asking "Why?" postponed things.

"Get going," she said.

Charlie kicked his truck because he felt angry.

"Start with the toys," she said, "and put them away. You're always helping me, so I'll help you."

Charlie picked up the truck and the airplane and the dinosaur book and the puzzle pieces all over the place and the crayons and the coloring book.

His mother picked up the lost sock under the couch, the sneakers, and the stuffed frog in the middle of the floor, the cowboy hat on the chair, and the half a cookie on the table.

"Presto, chango, the mess is gone," she said. "See, that wasn't so bad. It only took a minute."

"It's not so bad when somebody helps," said Charlie.

"You're right about that," said his mother.

Nancy McArthur is a free-lance writer who lives in Cleveland and teaches journalism at Baldwin-Wallace College. She has written articles for "Harper's," "Cleveland Magazine," and the Cleveland "Plain Dealer," and a book, "How To Do Theatre Publicity" (Good Ideas Company).

My Day

By Adele Schwarz

I must tell someone about my first day at school.

I woke up and I began to dress.

None of the socks in my drawer matched.

My dress ripped under the arm.

I had to wear my sweater. It itches.

The hem was hanging from my skirt.

I had to hunt for a safety pin.

In the mirror I saw my hair curling up instead of under.

My sister was in the bathroom with the door locked.

I had a stomachache.

At breakfast my brother grabbed my Snoopy place mat.

I dribbled milk on my sweater. The spot got bigger as I rubbed.

My mom said I had to carry an umbrella to school.

I was the only kid with an umbrella.

There are two teachers in the second grade.

I got the one who puts kids in the closet. Everybody says so.

My seat is in the back of the room behind the tallest boy in the class.

It is next to the window and in front of the radiator.

The sun was in my eyes. I was broiling.

The girl next to me said mind your own business when she opened her desk.

The teacher told *me* to stop talking when the boy in front asked for a pencil. My face turned scarlet. Everyone noticed.

The teacher handed out new reading books. There were not enough to go around. I had to share with the girl next to me, the one who said I was nosy. She kept pulling the book closer.

She sneezed all over the page. I held my breath so I would not get the flu.

At lunch my sandwich was soggy from the smashed tomato.

The teacher saw me throw out my lunch.

In gym I had no sneakers. I had to watch.

In art we had to paint a picture of ourselves . . . with watercolors.

I look like I am melting.

The teacher did not hang it up. I will never be an artist.

On the way home Sammy pulled up my skirt. As I ran away from him, the button popped.

I fell on the sidewalk and got a bloody knee. I think the pebbles are still in it. My sister called me crybaby.

My mother said it could not hurt that much. She put *iodine* on it!

At dinner my dad said how was your first day at school.

I said it was okay. . . .

Adele Schwarz is a writer of short stories and children's books and is also a photographer-journalist. She lives in Shavertown, Pa.

This Is What I Know

By Denise Gosliner Orenstein

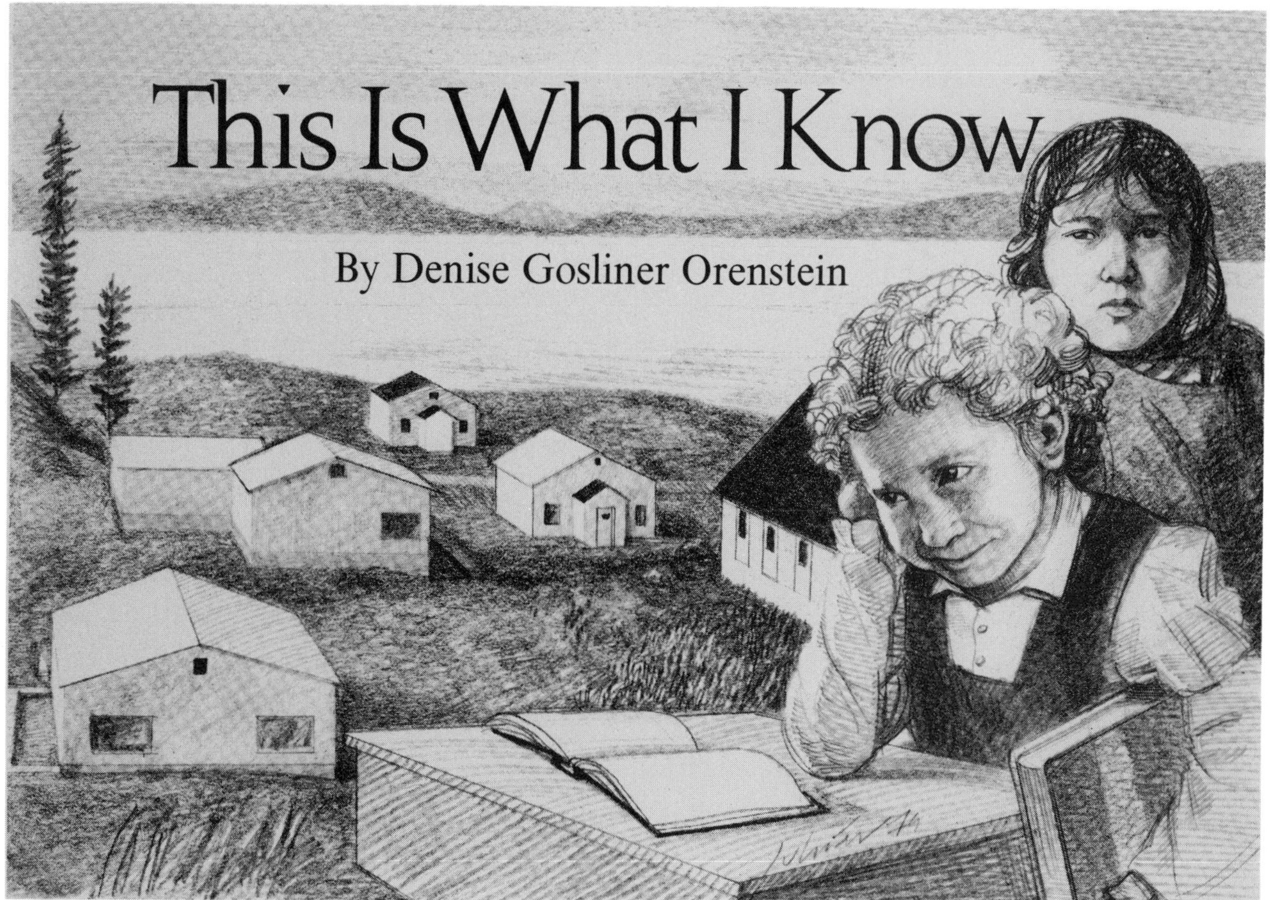

I haven't always lived here.

My mother is a teacher. Last summer, we moved from New York City to live on Klawak, an island in Alaska. This island only has small buildings. My mother says we will learn a new way of life. I don't know about that.

My name is Shawn. My hair is red and curly. When we first moved to this island, everyone stared. I thought they stared because my hair is red. I hate my hair.

I guess you know what an island is like. It's a piece of land with water all around. This island kind of sits in the middle of the ocean. My mother says I shouldn't say "kind of." It's not good English.

I learned a bunch of other things when I moved here too. Like how to clean a fish without feeling funny and slimy. And how to find salmonberries in the spring. My friend Vesta taught me that. And how to blow bubbles in my milk. I taught myself that.

I want to tell you about my friend Vesta. Her hair is short and dark. She knows how to tie three different kinds of rope knots with her eyes closed, and she can hop backward on ice without slipping. Vesta is a Tlingit Indian. I'm not. My mother says I'm Caucasian, but I can't pronounce that. The kids at school say I'm white. I can pronounce that.

This is what I know: there are five kinds of Native people living in Alaska. "Native" means people who have always lived in a place. The five kinds of Native people are Eskimo, Athabascan, Haida, Aleut, and Tlingit. You pronounce the word "Tlingit" like this: Klinget. I don't know why.

My friend Vesta has a grandfather who loves me. It wasn't always like that. I used to be scared of Vesta's grandfather because he was so old and quiet, and sometimes his hands shook. When I visited Vesta's house, her grandfather would stare at me. I thought he didn't like me because my hair was red. This is how I felt when I first moved to Klawak and met Vesta's grandfather: I was sad. I missed New York City and my friends from my New York school. There's a lot of sky and water around Klawak, and I don't know what to do with it all. It rained a lot. My hair got curlier. I couldn't wear my sneakers because my feet got wet and muddy. My mother bought me a pair of ugly green boots. I felt lonely. Sometimes when I'm lonely, I stop being nice. I stir my cereal around and around until it gets cold and then I won't eat it. I stick gum under my desk at school and won't look at the teacher. I won't make my bed and I won't brush my hair. My mother says sometimes I'm irritating.

Vesta was the only one at school who was nice to

me. My teacher was all right, but that didn't count because she was old and had to be nice. Vesta sat next to me in class and lent me her red pen. One day, she invited me to visit her house after school. That made me feel better.

At Vesta's house, her mother made us a special drink called Russian Tea. This is what Russian Tea tastes like: Christmas. Vesta says that Russian Tea is made from oranges, cinnamon, and many other spices. She says that once, Russian people lived in Alaska and some lived in Klawak.

Russian Tea makes your nose run, but there's usually a napkin around.

We were drinking Russian Tea when Vesta's grandfather came in. He was carrying a walking stick and wore a brown parka. It had a hood like my jacket. He was tall. He walked slowly, looked at me, but didn't speak. My hair started to feel very red. I decided to go home.

The next time I saw Vesta's grandfather, I was in John Petrovitch's store. Mr. Petrovitch has a Russian name. Maybe he is related to some Russians who used to live here. I like going to Mr. Petrovitch's store because it is different from any store I've ever seen in New York City. It's full of all kinds of things like crackers and camera film and flannel shirts and dried fish.

I nodded to Vesta's grandfather when I came in the store, and pulled up my jacket hood to cover my red hair.

Vesta's grandfather looked at me but didn't move. "Hello, Shawn," Mr. Petrovitch said. "What can I do for you?" I stared at my ugly green boots. Somehow I felt strange in front of Vesta's grandfather. Mr. Petrovitch and Vesta's grandfather were looking at me. I pulled on the strings of my jacket hood. "Shawn?" Mr. Petrovitch said.

I knew I had to speak. "Mr. Petrovitch," I said, looking down, "my mother needs some lettuce and powdered milk."

This is what I know: no one in Klawak drinks regular milk from a carton. Milk comes from cows, and there are no cows in Klawak.

If the people in Klawak had milk sent from the lower states, the milk would go sour on the long, long trip. There's a kind of milk that is all dried up. It looks like soap flakes. This is powdered milk. It never goes sour. When you mix it with water, it almost tastes like fresh milk. Sometimes I think I know a lot.

"Well, Shawn," Mr. Petrovitch said, "I'll be happy to sell you some milk, but the lettuce is no good. It froze on the way up from Seattle."

Sometimes the weather in Alaska is so cold, things freeze quickly. Since the Klawak soil doesn't have the right minerals for vegetables to grow, we order lettuce and things like that from a city called Seattle. Seattle is in a state called Washington. When the weather is real cold, the vegetables we get from Seattle freeze before we can eat them. It's a long trip from Seattle. We hardly ever eat fresh vegetables any more. We eat canned food a lot because food in cans never freezes or goes bad.

"Okay, Mr. Petrovitch," I said, looking down at my boots, "I'll just take the milk."

All this time, Vesta's grandfather was quiet, but I could feel him looking at me. I figured he didn't like me very much. All the way home, I wondered why.

Now, this is the part that gets surprising. At least, I didn't expect what happened to happen. Vesta moved away to another town. Her father got a job in a cannery in a place called Ketchikan. Vesta and her mother had to go to Ketchikan too.

This is what I know: there are a lot of fish in Alaska. Many people all over the state go fishing for a living. That's their regular job. All the fish that are caught are sent to places across the United States. A cannery is a place where fish are cleaned and put into cans to be sent away. Vesta's father went to work in one of those canneries.

My mother said Ketchikan wasn't very far, and I would see Vesta again soon. I didn't care about soon. I wanted Vesta to be around *now*. I told my mother that I hated Alaska and hated Klawak and hated fish. I probably was being irritating.

After Vesta left, nothing was the same. No one in school whispered with me or passed me notes and funny drawings. No one in school invited me to their homes. No one gave me Russian Tea. My hair grew longer. I left my bed unmade a lot.

One day, when I came home from school, my mother called me into the kitchen. She was making deer stew. Sometimes people call it "venison." I don't know why.

"Shawn," my mother said, stirring the stew with a big wooden spoon, "I made some stew for Vesta's grandfather. With the family away, he needs a little looking after."

I didn't say anything. Vesta's grandfather seemed old enough to look after himself. My mother put the spoon down.

"I'd like to give some of this stew to Vesta's grandfather for dinner. I think he would appreciate a hot meal."

I looked away. I knew what was coming.

"Shawn," my mother continued, "would you please take a bowl of the stew over to Vesta's grandfather's house after school tomorrow?" I pulled at my hair. A bunch of curls were stuck in a big knot.

"Why do I have to?" I asked.

"I just finished telling you, Shawn," Mother said very slowly. "Vesta's grandfather is living all alone. He's an old man and can hardly cook a big meal for himself. It seems to me that you would want to do something for your friend's grandfather."

I bit my lip. "Well, I don't," I said. And then I ran out of the room.

My mother says that sometimes I can be stubborn. My mother followed me into my room. I was lying on my bed with my head under the pillow. My mother sat down next to me and put her hand on my back.

This is what I know: my mother has soft hands. They feel good against your back if you just might cry.

"Honey," my mother said softly, stroking my back. "I know living here has been a big adjustment for you. I know that you're trying hard."

I took the pillow off my head and looked up. Maybe there were tears on my face. My mother put her arms around me and held me for a while. Sometimes I love my mother so much, my heart hurts.

That day, after school, I poured a bunch of deer stew into a bowl. I wondered whether the bowl was big enough. Vesta's grandfather might eat a lot. Next I covered the bowl with tinfoil so it wouldn't fall out while I was walking. I sat down and stared at the bowl of deer stew for a long while.

I might have felt a little scared.

When I knocked on Vesta's grandfather's door, no one answered. I knocked again, then pushed the door gently. It opened halfway.

"Hello," I said softly. "Hello," I said again, louder. I looked inside. Vesta's grandfather was sitting at the kitchen table, cutting a piece of wood with a knife. He didn't look up. I walked into the house and put the bowl of stew on the table for Vesta's grandfather.

"My mother and I thought you might like some deer stew," I said. "My mother made it. Some people call deer 'venison.' I don't know why."

Vesta's grandfather reached out and touched the bowl with his fingertips. And then he looked up.

This is what I know: Vesta's grandfather's face is different from any other face I've seen. His skin is the color of wood, the lines on his face like the grain of wood. The eyes are very dark, very large, and very still. I held my breath.

Vesta's grandfather looked beautiful to me. I'm not sure why.

Vesta's grandfather put one hand on my arm and pointed to a chair.

"Sit down," he said. Vesta's grandfather had never spoken to me before. I sat down next to him. He picked up the piece of wood again and began cutting it with a knife. I had seen other men in Klawak cut wood like that. It's called carving. It's a kind of artwork. Vesta's grandfather began to talk as he carved. This is what he said:

"This wood is like the pulse of a wrist. It's full of motion and warm inside the hand. What I am carving is alive." I watched the piece of wood change shape as Vesta's grandfather carved. It looked like magic. All at once, I could see the shape of a small, curved paddle. Suddenly, I wasn't scared of Vesta's grandfather any more.

"Are you carving a paddle?" I asked Vesta's grandfather. →

He nodded and said: "This is a paddle like those from long ago. All we had in those days were paddles to move our boats. We had no engines. Even then, we carved our paddles like pieces of art. When I was small, like you, my uncle taught me to carve as I am carving now. He handed down what he knew. My uncle was an artist from way back, and taught me not to do anything halfway. The Tlingit people treat art as something alive, something to be respected."

"Have you ever carved a totem pole?" I asked Vesta's grandfather.

This is what I know: a totem pole is a tree without any branches. The bark is carved with all kinds of animals and painted all different colors. There are a lot of totem poles in Klawak. Vesta's grandfather nodded. "The totem pole here in Klawak," he said, "the one with the fox on top? I carved that."

I couldn't believe it. The fox totem pole was my favorite. Vesta's grandfather continued talking: "A person making totem poles has learned to study the animals. First, I had to study the fox. The fox is a lively creature, and runs around like a small child. The fox is the symbol of a child." He smiled and touched my hair. "Your hair is red, the same color of fox. You are lively and fast like the small animal the Tlingit people admire."

I was beginning to think that Vesta's grandfather didn't dislike me any more.

"What do the other totem pole animals mean?" I asked Vesta's grandfather.

He was quiet for a moment and then he said: "The crab is the symbol of the thief because he has so many hands. The mosquito represents teaching. When a mosquito bites, you start itching. Sometimes learning hurts."

"Did you paint the totem poles you carved?" I asked. "Totem poles are so big, so tall, how did you reach way up to paint them?"

Vesta's grandfather laughed. "You paint the totems when they are lying down across the ground," he said, "before they are placed upright to stand in the sky. Long ago, we used paintbrushes made from wild bushes, and made all different kinds of paints from nature around us. Some paints were made from tree bark, some from blueberries and blackberries. These old Indian paints last for hundreds of years. They never fade in the sun. Now, these paints from long ago are gone. Very few people remember them."

Vesta's grandfather put the paddle on the table next to the bowl of deer stew. It was finished. Vesta's grandfather looked at me.

"This paddle is for you," he said. "Take it home."

I felt funny. The paddle was so beautiful. I didn't feel right taking Vesta's grandfather's paddle home. He picked up the paddle and handed it to me. It felt warm, warm from the heat of his hands.

Vesta's grandfather looked at me. "The Tlingit does not turn down any gift," he said, "but accepts it with open arms."

That is when Grandfather and I became friends.

Yesterday, I saw the first Klawak snow. The wind was so cold, I wore long underwear to keep my skin from hurting. My mother made me a red hat with pointed earflaps. She says it goes with my red hair. When the wind blows on my way home from school, I like to tie my hat tightly and feel my warm hair curl against both ears.

Now I bring Grandfather his dinner every Friday afternoon. Sometimes he tells me stories from the time that he was young. Sometimes we carve animals out of warm, soft wood. Sometimes we eat Tlingit candy made from green seaweed and sugar. Sometimes we eat too much and our stomachs hurt.

This is what I know: in the late afternoon, the Klawak sky turns pink. If you walk up the hill behind the school yard, you can see totem poles shine in the moving light. Stand under the one with the red fox on top. Hold your breath. Hear the sounds from long ago.

Denise Gosliner Orenstein lived and taught in Alaska for several years, working as director of an orphanage and professor and traveling teacher. Her first children's novel, When the Wind Blows Hard, *was published in 1982.*

Text by Joan Lowery Nixon/Illustrations by Susan Faiola

There was me, Judy.
That's one.

And my mother and father.
They made two.

And together we made three.

Then my mother took me out for ice cream and told me that she and my father were getting a divorce, and she was marrying a wonderful man named Frank.

My father told me I could visit him on holidays.

One father, two fathers.

That made four.

After the divorce, my mother married Frank, and we moved into his house.

Frank had a son who parked his big motorbike in his bedroom, and popped his chewing gum, and never spoke to me.

Mother said we'd be such a happy family.

That made five.

My father took me out for ice cream and told me he had met a wonderful woman named Gloria, and he was going to marry her. Gloria wanted to be my mother too.

One mother, two mothers.

That made six.

Gloria had a little boy who said "NO!" to everything and kicked people on their legs. He could always find where the crayons were hidden, and he scribbled on the walls and on the bathroom mirror, and on the new overnight case Frank gave me.

My father said it made him so happy that we could all be together.

That made seven.

Gloria's brother lost his job, and he moved in. Every day he lay on the floor with a pillow under his head and watched all the game shows and soap operas on television.

My father and Gloria didn't laugh as much as they usually did.

That made eight.

When my mother brought me back to Frank's house, she told me I'd have a big surprise.

Frank's married daughter had left her husband and come home to live with them.

That made nine.

And she said Frank's daughter had a darling baby girl, and I could play with her.

Frank's daughter stayed in her room and cried a lot. She told me I could be the baby-sitter, and she gave me a quarter.

The baby was a nice baby, but she was always wet.

That made ten.

My mother got a lot of headaches.

She didn't smile much, and most of the time Frank had to go out of town on business.

One day my father took me out for ice cream.

He told me that his company had transferred him to South America. It was a big promotion, and besides that, it would be nice to get away from Gloria's brother. The only problem was that we wouldn't get to see

each other for a couple of years, and he hoped I'd understand.

Ten . . . take away four.
That made six.

Then my mother took me out for ice cream.

She said she and Frank had made a mistake, and were going to get a divorce.

Six . . . take away four.
That made two.

She told me she had rented an apartment and had got a job and would be home every day when I got home from school.

She said she needed me as much as I needed her.

She said we would be together, the two of us.

I was so glad my mother told me that.

Three was the best number.
Two will still be a good number.
But one would have been an all alone number.

One is me, Judy

Joan Lowery Nixon is the author of more than 50 award-winning children's books, including one that received the "best juvenile mystery" award from the Mystery Writers of America.

I Like You To Make Jokes with Me, But I Don't Want You To Touch Me

By Ellen Bass

Illustrated by Nancy Lawton

When my mommy goes shopping, she takes me with her. I like to push the cart. I put Snoopy up in the seat part so he can ride and I put my bottle up there with him. He likes apple juice.

I pick out the potatoes and drop them in the bag Mommy holds open. I pick out the onions and oranges too. They're all on low shelves.

Sometimes I see Jack in the store. He can juggle. He juggles oranges. Sometimes he lets me push the button on the cash register. And if Mommy gives me a bunch of grapes to eat before they get weighed, he teases me, "Hey, honey bunch. I see you munch."

Sometimes, though, he comes too close to me. He's big and his hands are big and I get scared.

One time, when we were joking, he tickled me and I ran crying, "Mommy, Mommy!" I snuggled my face in her neck and cried and cried.

Jack came after me and I heard Mommy telling him, "She got scared."

"Of me?" he asked, laughing. "Why, I'm just a silly old man."

Mommy was holding me and stroking my back. I stopped crying and peeked up from her shoulder.

"I'm just a silly old man," Jack said. "You don't have to be afraid of me."

I thought that was funny—silly old man—and I said silly old man lots of times that day. I just kept thinking about Jack and silly old man and his funny jokes and how I didn't like him to get close to me.

When we got home and Mommy was putting away the groceries, she said, "Sara, if you want to, next time we go shopping you can tell Jack that you like him to make jokes with you, but you don't want him to touch you."

I said, "You do it, Mommy." I didn't think I could.

So she turned toward the refrigerator and said, "I like you to make jokes with me, but I don't want you to touch me."

I thought that was funny—Mommy talking to the refrigerator. I laughed and said, "Do it again."

And she did. She said, "I like you to make jokes with me, but I don't want you to touch me."

"Again," I said.

And she said it again and again and again and again. "I like you to

make jokes with me, but I don't want you to touch me." I was laughing and squealing, she was so funny talking to the refrigerator.

Then she smiled at me and said, "You do it now." And I did. I told the refrigerator, "I don't want you to touch me, but I like to make a joke with you."

I did it lots of times too. And each time Mommy said, "That's good, Sara."

After all the groceries were put away, we ate peaches and pretzels for a snack.

The next time we went shopping, Jack was putting out little green cartons of strawberries and I wanted some strawberries too. But I was scared. I didn't want to get too close to him even though Mommy was right next to me.

She held my hand, leaned down to my ear and whispered, "You can say, 'I like you to make jokes with me, but I don't want you to touch me.' "

Just then he looked over at me and grinned, "Hi. How're you doing?"

I said, kind of quietly, "I don't want you to touch me, but I like to make a joke with you."

His face looked like he didn't understand. "You don't want me to touch you when you're making a joke with me?" he asked.

Mommy explained. She said, "She doesn't want you to touch her, but she likes you to joke with her."

"Oh," he said, and he nodded his head and raised his eyebrows, looking out over the strawberries. Then he said, "Oh," again and looked at me and Mommy and said, "That's okay. I can understand that."

Mommy smiled and took a carton of strawberries and gave me two, one for each hand.

Yesterday we went shopping again. At first I didn't see Jack. "Where is he?" I asked Mommy.

"I don't know," she said. "Maybe he's in the back and he'll be up front soon. Or maybe he has a day off." She was scooping tortilla chips into a bag.

"Can I have some?" I asked her. She handed me a few.

"No," I said, "I mean in a bag. I want a bag too."

"Okay," she said and scooped some chips into a little bag for me.

"Thanks," I said.

"You're welcome," she said.

I took my bag and walked all around the store, but I didn't see Jack.

After Mommy had paid for all the food and was picking up the bags, I saw him.

"Hi," I said.

"Hi there. How're you doing today?" He smiled at me. He was humming.

I looked up at Mommy. "He didn't touch me," I said.

"Of course I didn't touch you," he laughed. "You told me not to."

I thought about that for a minute. Then I smiled. I felt strong. And when I looked back up at Mommy she was beaming.

Ellen Bass has published several books of poetry, including For Earthly Survival, *which won the Elliston Book Award. She co-authored* No More Masks! An Anthology of Poems by Women *and* I Never Told Anyone, *an anthology of writings by survivors of child sexual abuse, as well as a collection of poems,* If We Gather. *She teaches "Writing about Our Lives" workshops for women.*

MY BROTHER STEVEN IS RETARDED

TEXT BY
HARRIET LANGSAM SOBOL

PHOTOGRAPHS BY
PATRICIA AGRE

My name is Beth, and I'm 11. I have a retarded brother, Steven. He's mentally retarded. He's older than I am, but he acts like he's younger. He's even smaller than I am. His body doesn't seem to grow the way mine does.

My mother explained "retarded" to me when I was very little. "Retarded" means you can't learn or understand things like everyone else. She said Steven's brain was damaged while he was being born, and that's why he can't do the things I can do. I used to think that "retarded" was catching, and I was afraid to stand next to Steven.

Then I thought maybe it was my mother's fault he was retarded, since he grew inside her before he was born. Now I know it's not catching, and I know it's not my mother's fault. If someone in our family has to be retarded, I'd rather it were Steven than me. Maybe that's not very nice, but it's true anyway.

I guess I love Steven because he's my brother, but many times I think he's hard to love. He doesn't look the same as other children, and he makes funny noises and sort of talks funny. He doesn't always use the right word for things, and because he mumbles it's hard to understand him.

He's kind of clumsy, and once in a while he knocks things over. When he breaks things or makes messes and I have to help my mother clean up, I get angry at him. Then I really feel bad because it's not his fault his brain was hurt.

On school days, Steven takes a bus to a special school for retarded children. He learns things like how to set

a table and how to go shopping at a grocery store. He has a good time there and has fun with his friends.

I wish Steven could do more for himself so my mother and father wouldn't have to spend so much time with him. I don't get to be alone with my parents as much as I'd like because they always seem to be busy with Steven. When my father does have free time, he and I like to walk our dog Smokey together.

My mother says that people don't know what's wrong with Steven. They notice that he's different, and they're curious and nervous and even a little bit scared. She says that's why they stare and giggle. All I know is that it makes me feel embarrassed, and I don't like that feeling. I guess I feel worst when other kids tease me and say that I'm retarded like Steven. And then I wonder why Steven is the one that's retarded and I'm not.

Before one of my friends comes to my house to play, I explain what "retarded" means so she won't be nervous or afraid of Steven. It gives me a good feeling when a friend comes along with me to take Steven for a walk.

It's easy to make Steven laugh, and when we play our own special ball game or

I tickle him, he seems to have such fun. Then I feel good. He's so happy when I spend time with him.

Steven and I were very proud the day he finally learned to spell his name out loud. We had been working on it for such a long time.

Lots of times I feel sorry for Steven. My mother and father say that they feel sorry that he's retarded, too. They say we will always be sad about it, but there really is nothing anyone can do to change it.

At night when I go to bed, I think about what will happen to Steven when he grows up. I know he will always be retarded. He will grow taller, but he will never act like other grown-ups. He won't ever be able to live alone and take care of himself like I will.

I hope he will be happy.

Harriet Langsam Sobol and Patricia Agre have collaborated on eight books. Sobol is a free lance writer. She has three children, the eldest of whom is retarded. Agre is a free lance photographer who is also the mother of three.

INSIDE OUT

I live in a crowded house. One day, I wanted something in that house, so I went outside to get it.

I live in a crowded house.

One day, I wanted something in that house, so I went outside to get it.

I sat down on the front porch and waited. I'm a very patient person, as well as being very intelligent. I knew that, soon enough, I would get just what I wanted.

In a few minutes, my two kid brothers came out of the crowded house and sat on the porch beside me. They are twins, and they make twice as much of a crowd as anyone else in the family.

"Hey, Maggie, what are you doing out here?" asked Robin.

Yeah, what?" asked Robert.

I took off my glasses and polished them. "I am looking for something inside the house?" I said quietly.

"Then why are you sitting out *here*?" asked both the boys.

"Because."

The two boys looked at one another. They know me, and they know what "because" means when I say it. They decided to play things my way.

"Can we try to guess what you want in the house?" Robert asked this time.

I am a reasonable person. "Sure," I said, putting on my glasses again.

So the twins started to guess.

Was it a book? No. A kite? No. The dog? No. Was it animal, vegetable, or mineral? No, no, no.

The twins gave up. Robert thought it would be wise to get some help. He went up to the front door and hollered, "Becky!"

Becky is our older sister. She's 14 and wears curlers a lot. When she came to the door, she was winding one up in her hair.

"What's the matter?" she asked.

"Come out here and help us guess what Maggie's looking for," said Robin.

Becky finished rolling up her hair, shrugged her shoulders, and sat down on the porch with everyone else. Now the porch was getting crowded. Becky's curlers alone took up a lot of space.

"Okay," she started. "It it animal, vegetable, or mineral?"

By Dagmar Guarino

"We already *asked* that!" yelled both the boys at the same time. Being twins, they did that a lot.

"Okay, okay, give me a chance," Becky said quickly. "Hmm . . . is it bigger than a bread box?"

"No," I said very seriously, trying to hide a giggle.

Becky tried some more questions. Did it hop? Could it sing? Did it wear tennis shoes?

I said no to everything.

Finally Becky gave up too. She went to the door and called, "Hey, Mom!"

Our mother came outside with paint on her hands. She likes to do still lifes, and her oil paints are forever crowding up the house.

"What is it?" she asked.

"Would you help us try to guess what Maggie wants in the house," Becky said.

"Okay," said Mom, as she squeezed into a spot near one end of the porch.

"Is it round?"

"No."

"Square?"

"No."

"Could I paint it?"

"I don't think so," I said smugly.

My mother frowned for a moment. Finally she went to the door and said. "This is all very interesting. Let's give your father a chance at it. Peter!"

Then Dad came running out from the kitchen, a finger to his lips. He was always baking things, and his fattening desserts didn't help to thin out the crowded conditions much.

"*Ssh,* not so loud," he said. "I've got cake in the oven."

"Hey, Dad, try and guess what Maggie wants in the house," said Robin.

"My cake?" asked Father, settling down on the opposite end of the porch. He was disappointed when I said no. Usually I just love his cakes.

He tried other things. Bananas? Ice cream? Root beer?

But no, it wasn't any of these things.

"Well, I give up," my father said, looking across the crowd of children at our dog, who was pretty good herself at crowding up the house with chewed-up slippers. Shce climbed up on Becky's knee and went to sleep. The rest of the family just sat on the porch of the empty house, staring at me and thinking.

At last I squeezed myself out of the crowd and stood up. I guess I must have looked pretty pleased with myself.

"Do all of you really want to know what I wanted inside the house?" I asked, opening the front door.

"Yes!" shouted the whole family, turning to look at me. "What did you want?"

"*PRIVACY!*" I said as I stepped inside the empty house and locked the door. "Privacy!" I repeated—and I laughed.

And for the first time ever, I got some.

Dagmar Guarino, twenty-eight, lives and writes in New York City. "Inside Out" was her first published story.

No Job for MOM

BY ANITA GOLDWASSER

One day a few months ago, my Mom came home from work with teary-looking eyes. She plopped down on the couch and put her feet up.

"Did you hurt yourself?" I asked.

Mom shook her head, "No, I lost my job."

"Were you fired?"

"No. People are fired for not doing their jobs right," she explained. "But if

the company doesn't have enough work to keep someone busy, they tell the person she's not needed any more and they call it a layoff. Other people were laid off too. Ten of us are out of work now."

I felt sorry to see Mom unhappy, but deep down, I was sort of glad. If Mom wasn't going to her job, that meant she could spend more time at home. Ever since Mom and Dad got divorced and I started first grade, Mom had been working at this factory. She left the house at 6 A.M.—even before I woke up. My brother Dan made breakfast (and sometimes burned the toast). Then he'd walk me to my school and go on to his class at Junior High.

After school Dan visited his friends. I was too scared to stay home alone, so I'd go to a neighbor's house 'til Mom picked me up. But this year, when I went into fifth grade, I began staying home alone. Sometimes I hung around the school yard, or my friend Angela and I played kickball.

Now, I thought, Mom will be home *every* day. She'll even be there for breakfast. This layoff was beginning to sound like a terrific idea.

Mom started talking again. "We're not going to have much money for a while."

Oh, I hadn't thought of that. "You mean no movies or going to roller skating rinks and things like that?" I asked.

Mom nodded. "And no new clothes—and no vacation this year. We can't afford it."

"I've got seven dollars in the bank. Do you want that?" I offered.

She kissed me. "No—keep saving that for your leathercraft set. We'll be getting some money each week."

"How—if you're not working?" I asked.

"There's something called Unemployment Insurance that will help out," Mom explained.

Big words like those always get me mixed up, but Mom continued: "When people lose their jobs, the government gives them money to live on. The amount you get depends on where you live and how much money you used to earn on your job. Here in California, I'll get eighty-six dollars a week, since I used to earn about two hundred. The eighty-six dollars will help us buy food and pay the rent. I'm also going to see if we can get food stamps."

I told Mom I remembered seeing a woman at the supermarket give the cashier something that looked like phony money. "Were those food stamps?" I asked.

"Yes," said Mom. "The County Government gives them free to very poor people. People with a little

money can buy their food stamps. It's sort of like buying food at a discount. For example, some families pay twenty-five dollars and receive stamps that are good for fifty dollars worth of food. Then they go to the store and pay for whatever food they want with the stamps."

Pretty neat, I thought.

A few days later, Mom put on her jacket and said, "I'm going down to the Unemployment Office."

"Can I go with you?" I asked. I was curious.

"You'll be bored," she warned. "It may take a long time."

I wanted to go anyway—but the minute we walked into the Unemployment Office, I wished I had stayed home.

About a hundred people stood on long lines. Mom waited on one line for almost an hour before the clerk finally handed her some papers.

"Can we go home now?" I asked.

"Not yet," Mom said. She sounded tired. "After I fill out these forms, I'll have to stand on another line."

Wow, had I gotten myself in a fix. I could have been out in the fresh air playing with Angela. The room was filled with so much cigarette smoke that I kept coughing and my eyes itched. Another hour passed before Mom finished waiting on the second line.

"Did you get the money?" I asked, as we went out.

"It's not that easy," Mom replied. "First, someone has to check my papers and ask the company where I used to work if everything I said about the layoff is true."

"Don't they believe you?" I was surprised.

"I guess they're afraid some people will lie." She shrugged. "That's why they ask so many questions. People can't just come in, say they lost their jobs, and walk out with their pockets full of money."

I guess that's true. But I still thought it was mean to make people wait on line so long.

Two weeks went by before Mom started collecting the money from Unemployment Insurance. Now, every other week she waits on line at that same office to pick up her check.

We do lots of things differently now. We have more beans than before, and hardly any meat. I started getting free lunches at school. The first day, some kids pointed at me when I took the free lunch and whispered, "She's poor. That's why she doesn't pay for her food." I felt weird. I wanted to run out of the cafeteria, but I was too hungry to skip lunch.

When I got home I told Mom what had happened.

"I'm glad you stayed," she said quietly. "Just ignore the teasing. There's nothing wrong with accepting a little help when things are hard."

Dan and I help with our money too. Dan earns $22 a week delivering newspapers, and I walk our neighbors' dogs and wash their cars. Car-washing is the best. I charge $1.50 an hour or $2 for a whole car.

Last week we bought clothes for me and Dan at a rummage sale. We found some really neat shirts and jeans that cost only 25 cents each. I like them because they're soft, not stiff and scratchy like the new stuff.

Mom spends lots of time looking for a new job. Every morning she reads the "Classified Ads" in the newspapers. Those are the dull-looking pages full of words printed so small you practically need a magnifying glass to read them. No pictures at all.

Sometimes she'll say, "Here's a job I could try for." Then she writes to the company, or phones them. She hates it when some companies don't even answer her letters.

A few companies have asked her to come in for an interview. That's a meeting between the person looking for a job and a person who hires people. The woman or man she talks to is called a Personnel Manager, and they ask lots of questions about the kind of work Mom can do. Sometimes the Personnel Manager interviews dozens of people even though only one can be hired. At first Mom was kind of excited about going out for interviews. But since she hasn't had any luck finding a job in all these months, she's gotten very discouraged.

"Will you get Unemployment Insurance forever if you can't find a job?" I asked her.

"No, they only give it to you for one year," she replied.

"What happens then?"

"If I can't find a job by that time, we'll have to go on Welfare."

Welfare. I'd heard the word lots of times, but now I thought I'd better understand what it means.

"How does Welfare work?" I asked.

"Well, " said Mom. "I'll have to talk to someone called a 'social worker' and explain why we need the money. They'll ask lots of questions and probably come to our house."

"In case we're lying?" I interrupted. "We might be secret millionaires, right?"

"Right," Mom laughed. "Then if the social worker approves us, the County Government will give us money to live on. But I hope I'll find a job before my Unemployment Insurance runs out."

I hope she does too. But I'm getting kind of used to having less money. For birthdays, I draw cards instead of buying them. I don't spend money for gifts, I make them. So far I've made a patchwork pillow stuffed with old stockings. Then I embroidered an "A" on it and gave it to my friend Angela for her birthday. I'm going to give Mom a plant I grew from a seed. It's doing beautifully in a sunny window at school. I know Mom'll love it. We still have fun on weekends—picnicking or bike-riding in the park. There are lots of great activities that don't cost money.

One thing really surprises me about all this. Even though Mom doesn't have a job now, we don't see each other that much because I'm in school or out playing and she's usually off looking for a job. I think she's more tired now than she was when she used to come home from work at the factory.

On my next birthday, I'll be 11. That's pretty old. It's not as though I'm still a baby who needs someone to cook meals and play with her all the time.

I hope Mom finds a job soon. I think she'll be happier. To tell you the truth, I think I'll be happier too.

Anita Goldwasser, a copywriter, is the author of Planning for Profits: The Retailer's Guide to Success.

THIS IS A PICNIC. . . .

THIS IS A PICNIC. . . .

THIS IS A PICNIC. . . .

THIS IS A PICNIC,
BECAUSE A PICNIC IS WHEN YOU
DON'T HAVE TO EAT AT THE TABLE.

THIS IS A SLEEP-OUT. . . .

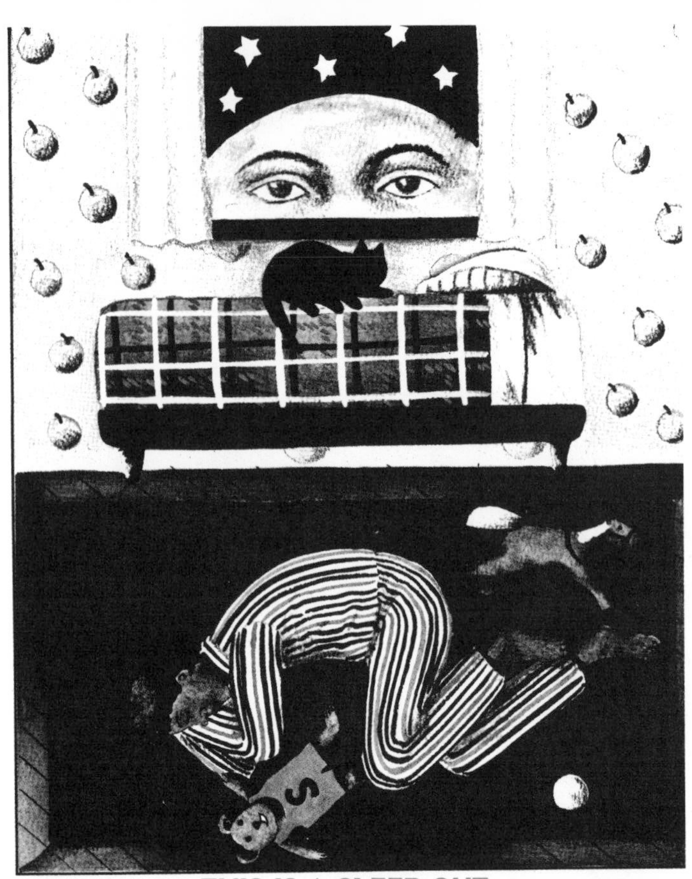
THIS IS A SLEEP-OUT. . . .

THIS IS A SLEEP-OUT. . . .

THIS IS A SLEEP-OUT,
BECAUSE A SLEEP-OUT IS WHEN YOU
DON'T HAVE TO SLEEP IN YOUR OWN BED.

THIS IS A PRESENT. . . .

THIS IS A PRESENT. . . .

THIS IS A PRESENT. . . .

THIS IS A PRESENT,
BECAUSE A PRESENT IS WHEN YOU DON'T
HAVE TO WAIT FOR A SPECIAL DAY.

THIS IS A VACATION. . . .

THIS IS A VACATION. . . .

THIS IS A VACATION. . . .

THIS IS A VACATION,
BECAUSE A VACATION IS WHEN YOU'RE NOT WHERE YOU USUALLY ARE.

Phyllis Rose Eisenberg is the author of A Mitzvah Is Something Special *and* Don't Tell Me a Ghost Story.

When Judy Died

by Ruth LuSan

I hate it when little kids die. Little kids aren't supposed to die. They're supposed to run around and scream and yell and cry and tell on each other.

My sister Judy died a year ago when I was nine. When it happened, all I did was get really mad. First at the man who hit her with his truck and then at God. Everyone kept telling me "God wanted Judy with Him." But why would He want that? Judy never went to church or prayed. I don't think He even knew her.

Judy was only six and really smart. She could read my brother Frank's books. (He's 12.) My dad always gets mad at Frank because Frank wants to be a helicopter pilot and not a lawyer like my dad. Once when I wanted a quarter, I said, "Guess what I want to be when I grow up, Daddy? A lawyer, just like you." Now whenever I want money he gives it to me. He calls me "*my* daughter." I think my momma knows what I'm up to because she just smiles whenever I do that.

I went with my parents to the funeral place. Frank stayed home and cried a lot. I only cried a little bit. I heard my dad crying in his room. My sister Janet came home from college and cried too. She told me that it's good to cry because then you won't get ulcers. The only one of us that didn't cry was my mother. I think she was mostly mad, like me.

I didn't like the funeral place. When we opened the door, all these bells started ringing and this man came out and said, "Can I be of service?" Real polite and softly like someone was asleep. My mother said, "Yes, we'd like to arrange a funeral." He said, "Certainly," and showed us his office.

While everyone was talking about caskets and flower arrangements, I was looking at the pictures on the wall. Everything in the whole building was beige except the carpet, which was green.

Suddenly I had to go to the bathroom so I asked the man where it was. He told me, and I half-ran because I had to go pretty badly. There were flowers all over the place and boxes of tissue. It was a pretty big building, and there was organ music coming from somewhere.

When I got back to the office, my parents were signing a lot of papers. Finally, everything was finished, and the funeral man shook hands with my mom and dad and gave me a nail file with the name of the funeral place on it.

It was 1:30 when we got home. We all sat in the living room and talked about Judy. No one wanted to go to school or work because they were afraid they would start to cry. I was glad I didn't go because it was math day. Judy was real good at math and always helped me with division. She was only in the first grade but she could add, subtract, multiply, *and* divide. My mom taught us to read and write and do math when we were really little. I can read and write, but that's all.

My sister Janet kept talking about Judy getting born and how funny-looking she was. Frank started crying again, and I started coloring my map of Australia. I really want to go there and drink beer like my dad did during the war. He was a typist in Sydney. My mom is a chemist, and they met in Cleveland.

My mom is a really good chemist. She has a lab downtown and sometimes lets us visit. My grandma made me and Frank and Janet white jackets like my mom and all the other chemists wear at the lab. Grandma was working on Judy's jacket, but she probably stopped when she found out that Judy died.

I was on the way to the kitchen when the phone started ringing. It was Jeannie P. Vincent.

"I heard your sister died," she said.

"Yeah. She got run over by a truck."

"Do you think Judy felt anything?"

"I don't know. They say she died pretty fast."

"Oh. Well, see you at school. Bye."

"Bye."

Jeannie P. Vincent is my best friend.

I came back into the living room. Frank wasn't crying any more. He was playing with his key chain. Once in a while a tear would come out, but he wasn't making any crying noises. Suddenly Janet asked when we were going to bury Judy. My father started telling us all the plans. He said that there would be a small service at the funeral place and then we would go to the cemetery. He told us that he would like to have the funeral tomorrow, but it was going to take a while for all the relatives to get here. So instead the funeral would be Friday.

We went out to dinner that night because no one felt like cooking. I had a hamburger and onion rings. Everyone else had steak.

On the way home, we stopped at the store and bought lots of paper plates because relatives are always eating, and no one wanted to wash dishes.

We got home at about 8:30, and everyone went to bed. Janet kept saying relatives take a lot out of you.

In the middle of the night, I got up to go to the bathroom, and I heard Frank crying again. I looked in his room but he wasn't there. He was in Judy's room.

"Hey, Frank. You okay?"

"No." He was sitting on the floor.

I opened the door wider and walked in. He was holding one of the model cars he and Judy built together.

"Come on, Frank. Grandma told me on the phone that Judy was in heaven," I said. He just cried harder. He was still in there when I went back to bed.

My mom drove me to school the next day. As I was getting out of the car, she asked me to go to Judy's class and get all of Judy's stuff. Then she handed me my note for being absent.

Judy's teacher, Mrs. Farley, got kind of shaky when she saw me. All the little kids didn't know what was going on, so they asked me where Judy was. I told them she died, and they said "Oh" and went back to their desks.

Mrs. Farley handed me some papers and books and Judy's orange sweater. She told me that she was sorry about Judy and walked me to the door.

When I got to my class, my teacher, Mr. Stoker, was all by himself correcting papers. Everyone else was in the library.

"Hi, Mr. Stoker. Sorry I'm late. My aunt came over and . . ."

"Do you have a note?"

"Yes. Here it is."

He took it and read it two or three times. Then he looked at me over his glasses and said, "It is important to carry on. Join the class at the library."

If your sister ever dies, don't go to school. People act weird. I walked into the library, and Jeannie P. Vincent came over and said hello. Everyone else just looked at me. Either that, or they said something dumb like "I hope it didn't hurt her too much." I don't think it hurt her too much because she was a bouncy sort of kid. Once she fell out of the tree in our backyard and just laughed. I fell out of the same tree and broke my arm.

So all day people got embarrassed and said dumb things. All the relatives were there

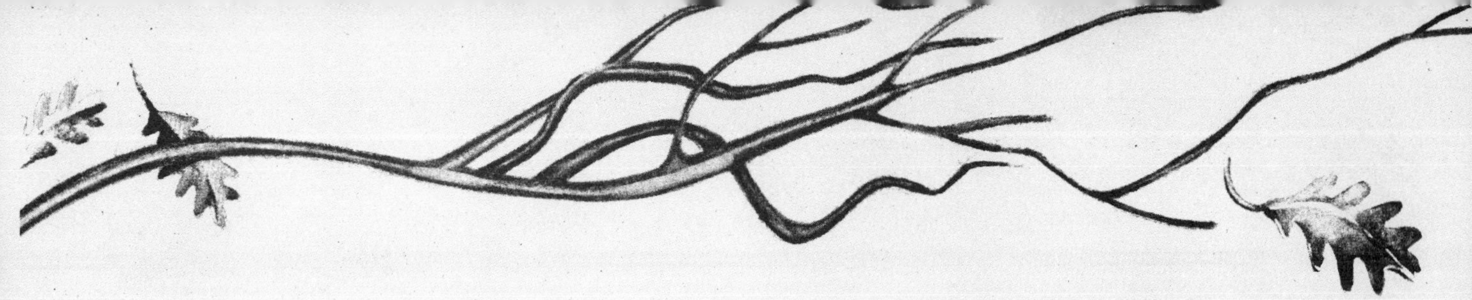

when I got home. People were crying and hugging and I thought I was going to be swallowed up.

During breakfast the next day, all the relatives started crying and hugging again. Luckily, a limousine came and took us to the funeral place. Lots of people from our neighborhood were there waiting for us.

Everyone went in and sat down. Two of the funeral people wheeled Judy's casket down the aisle. It was really small.

My cousin, who lives about a block from us and who is a minister, did the service. He told everyone that Judy was really nice and never did anything wrong. I guess he doesn't remember the time she put toothpaste in Frank's ear.

After he finished, everyone went outside. They put the coffin and a lot of flowers in a big black car called a hearse. Then everyone got in their own cars and followed the hearse out to the cemetery.

It took us about a half hour to get to the cemetery. There were 29 cars in the line. I counted them when we were on a big wide curve in the road. The cemetery was real quiet, and there were lots of trees. They dug Judy's grave under an oak tree, just like the one we fell out of. The grave scared me. Everyone told me that it wasn't really Judy going under the ground. They said that the real Judy would stay alive in our minds. The idea still scared me.

Uncle Paul and Aunt Joyce read out of the Bible while the rest of my uncles carried the coffin up the hill. Arthur, my minister cousin, said some prayers and then everyone sang Judy's favorite song, the "Battle Hymn of the Republic." Frank and me and Janet really started crying then because it was the song we all had taught her to sing in a big booming voice.

Everyone started back to their cars then. None of us were going to stay around and watch them actually bury the casket. Janet and me and Frank were walking back to the limousine when I looked back and saw my daddy and momma taking a rose from someone's wreath and putting it on the casket. My mom started crying then and I felt better. I didn't want her to get ulcers.

On the way home Janet told me that when you die you no longer feel sick, feel pain, or feel sad. I hope that's true because if it is, Judy has nothing to worry about.

Ruth LuSan has a B.S. in Mechanical Engineering from Tufts University. She wrote this story when she was seventeen.

STORIES FOR FREE CHILDREN®

NEW LIFE, NEW ROOM

BY JUNE JORDAN

Illustrated by Ray Cruz

On top of Momma's getting so big and so sleepy, the apartment was beginning to be small.

How was the apartment going to hold Mr. Robinson, Mrs. Robinson, Rudy, Tyrone, Linda, *and* a new Baby Brother, or a new Baby Sister?

"It'll be crowded," said Mr. Robinson, shaking his head. He looked over at his wife: "I wish the housing people would let us have a bigger place. I honestly do. But they don't let you have a reason to hope. They just tell you they're sorry."

"Well, I've been thinking," said Mrs. Robinson. "Linda can't go on sleeping in the living room. How about her moving in with the boys in our room, and we'll take the smallest room with the baby?"

"If that's the way it has to be, that's the way it'll be," answered Mr. Robinson. "We'll work it out."

At first, Linda had been very unhappy, years before, when she had to move out from her parents' bedroom, and when she had to take over the living-room couch as her own bed. But soon she learned how to open and close the couch easily. And then she got used to hanging her clothes in the hallway closet, or folding them for the bottom drawer of her mother's bureau, or pushing them into the skinny top drawer of her brothers' bureau. So she began to really like her place in the apartment. It was interesting to have parts of you spread out or hiding everywhere, all over the whole house.

And in some ways, the living room was the best because everybody came into it, every day, and because that was where the family would just sit, talking, or else dance, or else watch the TV. There was no loneliness in the living room. So it was a good part, and maybe the best part, of the house.

Her brothers, Rudy and Tyrone, liked Linda okay. But what about Linda's toys? Would she have to bring them into the new room?

Tyrone was worried. "Suppose she brings in the dolls, and the doll carriage, and the stove that doesn't even get hot or anything?"

"So?" answered Rudy, looking around. "How are they going to bother you? She can't help it if she's a girl and people keep giving her crazy presents like that."

Tyrone was quiet for a minute. Then he said, "Maybe we should make a deal."

"Like what?"

"Like no toys, no games, no nothing, unless all Three of us want to use it, you know. Nothing stays unless we can all use it for real."

"I don't know," said Rudy. "Linda is so little. And you and I don't even like the same things all the time."

"Well, but we could try, couldn't we?"

"We could try," answered Rudy.

Finally, Mr. and Mrs. Robinson called the children together. They said this and that. But mostly, Rudy, Tyrone, and Linda understood that Momma would have to leave for the hospital any minute: and while she was gone, they would all have to get ready, and help, and move things around, and lose places and trade places in the house.

It was going to be terrible. That was clear.

Then Mrs. Robinson left for the hospital, and by the next morning, the new baby, a new Baby Girl, had been born.

Mr. Robinson had been awake all night long, at the hospital. When the new Baby Girl was born, he was happy, and tired, and he took the day off from work. He felt he needed to celebrate, visit his wife, look at his new Baby Girl, take care of Rudy, Tyrone, Linda, move furniture, and sleep.

First he went to sleep. Then, when he woke up, he worked for two hours with a neighbor who was a friend of his. Together they pushed, pulled, lifted, turned, and made things bump, slide, roll, scrape, bang, and rock from one room to the other.

In the middle of this, the children came home from school.

They felt excited and scared and strange and crowded and lonely and pleased to see the terrific mess the two men were making in the house.

After Mr. Robinson stopped moving things and after he and his friend finished two beers, they left for the hospital. But just before he went out the door, Mr. Robinson tried to hug Rudy and Tyrone and Linda, in one big hug, with his huge, strong arms. But he couldn't quite do that, so he kissed each of them, in turn.

He said, "I'll be back soon, and I'll bring in some dinner by the time you're hungry . . . but meanwhile, why don't you go ahead and start trying out your new room?"

Now they were alone. The old apartment seemed new. Their new room looked too big. Rudy's narrow cot was up against one wall. Tyrone's narrow cot was on the other side of the room, against another wall. Where was Linda going to sleep? Between the cots, in the middle of the floor, was a trunk filled with toys. And next to the closet, their bureau looked big and lumpy and old.

All three children felt shy and small. Then Linda began running around. She brought all her toys and threw them on top of the trunk. Next she brought all her clothes out from every hiding place in the house and threw them on top of the toys.

Rudy went into action, and he began taking out the drawers from the bureau and dumping all of his and Tyrone's clothes on top of Linda's. Tyrone rushed after

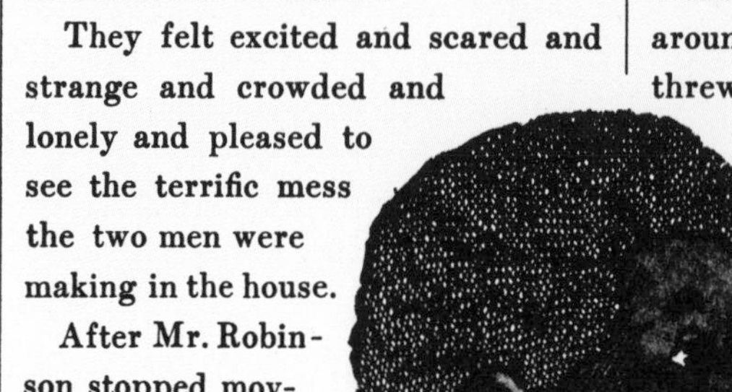

them, piling up games on top of clothes on top of toys on top of the trunk in the middle of the floor.

So the room began to look better. It didn't look too big any more. But the two beds were still far apart. You couldn't whisper from one bed to the other. So Tyrone and Rudy and Linda pulled the cots close by the mountain of things in the middle of the floor, and made the two cots into something like a long, low table.

There was hardly any time left. Today was when Linda would begin to sleep, as well as play, in the same room with her brothers. Then the next day Momma and the new Baby Girl would come home from the hospital.

Mr. Robinson bought a camp cot for Linda, and three jars of poster paint—yellow, red, and blue. Then, from his pockets he took out three thin paintbrushes. But under his chin, and inside his arms, was a gallon of chocolate ripple and strawberry ice cream, for the celebration.

Everybody was excited, and talking at once.

"What's the paint for?" asked Linda.

"I thought you kids would find something to do with it, in your new room," said Mr. Robinson.

"The windows!" shouted Tyrone. "We can paint the windows like a church or something!"

And they were off, painting, bumping, spilling, dabbing, dripping, poking, streaming, splashing, red and yellow and blue over the glass.

It got to be very interesting.

So the children slowed down, a bit, and began to move out of each other's way, so that red or yellow or blue could take its place on the windowpane and make shapes that were smiling, round, happy—large shapes of color that the sunlight would turn to warm and burning color rays like a rainbow bright over the whole room.

Rudy said, "Now let's get the toys and stuff sorted out and decide who gets to keep what, so we all can use all of the things, and then we can paint the top of the trunk too, if we feel like it."

So they scrambled into the great tumbling pile of things, and began to call out:

"Doll!"

"Throw!"

"Flashlight!"

"Keep!"

"Gun!"

"Throw!"

"Helmet!"

"Keep!"

"Stove!"

"Throw!"

"Tank!"

"Throw!"

"Magnets!"

"Keep!"

"Comic books!"

"Keep!"

"Dice!"

"Keep!"

"Rope!"

"Keep!"

"Blocks!"

"Throw!"

"Keep!"

"Throw!"

Linda wanted them thrown out. She wanted to get rid of everything babyish.

But Tyrone loved his blocks. "You just don't know what to do with blocks," he said. "You never built anything in your life!"

"You never let me," answered Linda.

"Well, now you can," Rudy observed. "We'll show you how. You could try building a house."

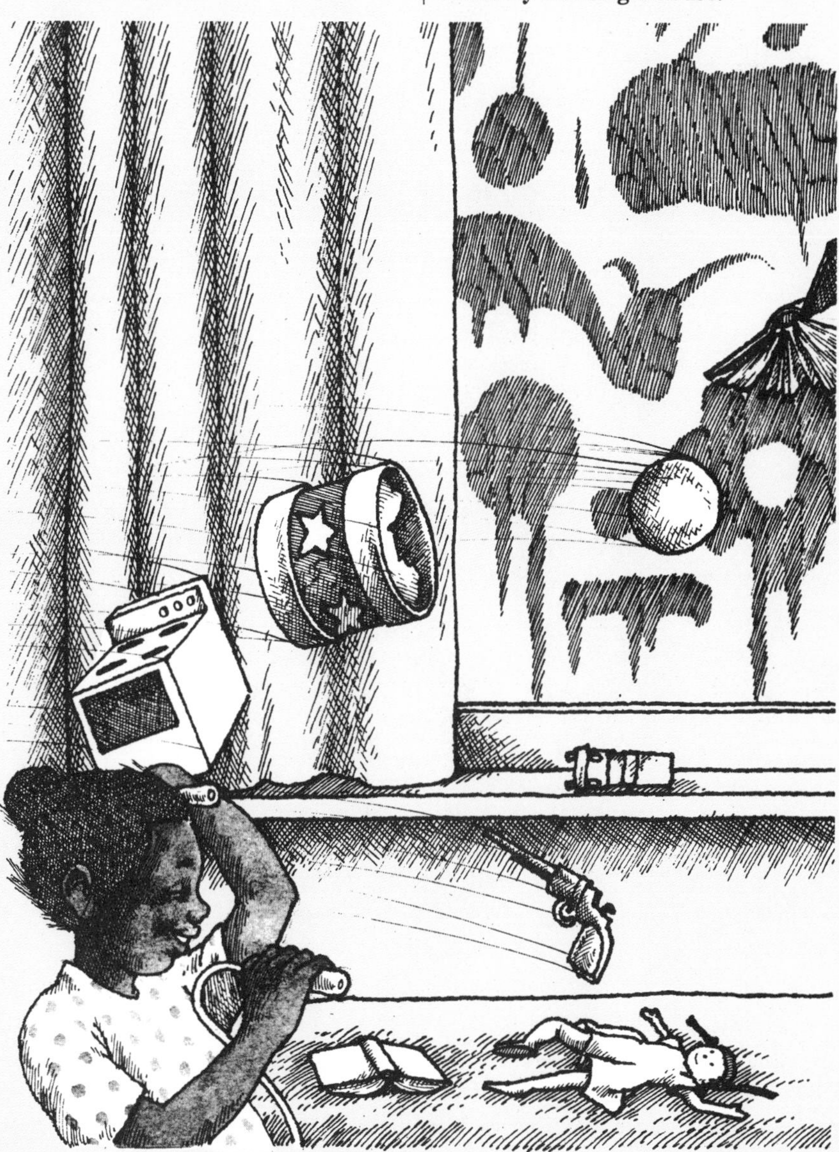

Linda said, "Do you know how to take care of a baby?"

"Oh, quit that," said Rudy. "A doll isn't anybody's baby."

"So what? Your blocks are make-believe too," she pointed out.

"Yeah. But what's more important. Building a bridge or taking care of a baby?" asked Tyrone.

"The baby," Linda said right away.

"What do you think?" Tyrone turned to Rudy.

But Rudy shrugged his shoulders and wouldn't say anything.

So Tyrone looked angry, but he kept quiet.

"I only want one doll," said Linda, sitting down, cross-legged, on the floor. "Just one. And you can play with her if you want."

Tyrone was making his mind up, slowly. At last he said, "That's the deal. All right. Keep the blocks and keep the doll. One doll."

So they went ahead, and finished sorting the toys. Then they made several trips down the hall to friends' apartments, and they threw out the things nobody wanted any more in the incinerator.

Now everything would fit inside the trunk.

And they closed it up, and painted three big, overlapping circles—red, yellow, and blue—to cover the whole top of the dark-green trunk.

Things were looking up.

"What about this big old bureau?" Tyrone asked aloud.

"Well, what about it?" asked Rudy.

"How can we hide it somewhere so we don't have to see it—so it's not sticking up ugly like that?"

At this moment, Mr. Robinson came into the room, and laughed, delighted with all the colors, and all the work done, so fast.

"Hey, you kids have done a great job here," he said. "Everything's going to be fine!"

"Tyrone wants to throw out the bureau," Linda said.

But nobody could talk Mr. Robinson into throwing out the whole bu-

reau, even though Rudy and Tyrone tried hard.

"I'll tell you what," said Mr. Robinson. "Leave the drawers out, but push them under the bed. One under each cot. That way they'll stay out of your way. And if you paint them different colors, you won't get them mixed up. How's that?"

Before anyone could answer, he carried the bureau frame out of the room, and out of sight.

So that solved the problem of the bureau that had been sticking up too high, too wide, and too ugly, in the new space of the new room.

"Tonight's a big night for you, isn't it," Mr. Robinson said in his deep voice. "You're all going to sleep in your new room for the first time. How about some strawberry and chocolate ripple ice cream, before you go to bed?"

At the table, Mr. Robinson asked the children what else they would like to have for the new room, and the children all said they would like something alive like goldfish or some baby plants that they could take care of, and help to grow.

It was like a party. A pajama party with ice cream and soda and Daddy and a brand-new room that would look like a rainbow in the morning.

When they got into bed, nobody said a word for two minutes. There was nothing but darkness. Somebody moved and made peculiar, quick noises. Then a flashlight went on, making a shadowy circle on the ceiling.

"I don't like it," Linda said.

"What?"

"The room. Everything's so far apart. How can we talk without Daddy hearing us? We'll get into trouble," said Linda.

"Well," Rudy said, "let's bring our cots together, over here by the windows, away from the door."

The children tiptoed around in the flashlight, and pulled the three cots together, side by side. But then they got the giggles again and started to tickle each other, and the cots began to slide and shake and pull apart. So Rudy got up and went to find some rope and Tyrone tied the beds together with the rope. And the three children snuggled together, on their new big bed, in their new big room, that was full of darkness.

Morning came with sunlight, and red and yellow and blue colors striped and circled the new room where the children lay, waking up, slowly.

It was a beautiful day. It was a beautiful room, very big, and open, and Rudy and Tyrone and Linda felt they were a bunch of lucky people—lucky to live together this way.

Rudy was not alone. Tyrone was not alone. And Linda was not alone. They were together in their own room. And they called it Our Room.

And Momma would be coming back today.

And a new *Baby Girl* was coming with her.

And everything was okay.

And everyone was ready.

June Jordan is the author of 14 books, most recently Passion, *a selection of her poetry;* Civil Wars, *a selection of her political essays; and* Kimako's Story, *a book for children. She is also Associate Professor of English at SUNY at Stonybrook, New York.*

Other books by Letty Cottin Pogrebin

Growing Up Free: Raising Your Child in the 80s
Getting Yours
How to Make It in a Man's World

About the Editor

Letty Cottin Pogrebin is a founder, editor and writer for *Ms.* magazine. She is the author of three previous books, most recently *Growing Up Free: Raising Your Child in the 80s.* She also served as an editor and consultant on the book, record and television special *Free to Be . . . You and Me,* and her work has been included in many anthologies relating to women's rights, family roles, sexism in education and nonsexist childrearing. Her next book is entitled *Family Politics: Love and Power on an Intimate Frontier.*

Ms. Pogrebin lives in New York City with her husband, two daughters and a son.

Editorial Assistants: Susannah Sheffer / Sue Zesiger / David Pogrebin

Additional Artistic Credits

"The Big Box"
Illustrated by Culverson Blair

"The Secret Soldier"
Illustrated by Elaine Grove

"A Gun Is No Fun"
Illustrated by Carlos Aguirre

"This Is What I Know"
Illustrated by Victor Juhasz

"My Day" and "Inside Out"
Designed by Robbin Schiff

"No Job for Mom"
Illustrated by Donna Corvi

"When Judy Died"
Illustrated by Andrew Rhodes

"Peachy Pig" and
"I Remember Grandma"
Designed by Diane Lamphron